50 DAYS OF
HEAVEN
RANDY ALCORN

A Tyndale nonfiction imprint

Visit Tyndale online at tyndale.com.

Visit Tyndale Momentum online at tyndalemomentum.com.

Tyndale, Tyndale's quill logo, *Tyndale Momentum*, the Tyndale Momentum logo, *The One Year*, and *LeatherLike* are registered trademarks of Tyndale House Ministries.

One Year is a trademark of Tyndale House Ministries. Tyndale Momentum is a nonfiction imprint of Tyndale House Publishers, Carol Stream, Illinois.

50 Days of Heaven: Reflections That Bring Eternity to Light

Copyright © 2006 by Eternal Perspective Ministries. All rights reserved.

Cover illustration of orange tree copyright © Nata_Alhontess/Shutterstock. All rights reserved.

Cover designed by Jen Phelps

Designed by Jessie McGrath

All Scripture quotations, unless otherwise indicated, are taken from the Holy Bible, *New International Version*,® *NIV.*® Copyright © 1973, 1978, 1984 by Biblica, Inc.® Used by permission. All rights reserved worldwide.

Scripture quotations marked NLT are taken from the *Holy Bible,* New Living Translation, copyright © 1996, 2004 by Tyndale House Foundation. Used by permission of Tyndale House Publishers, Carol Stream, Illinois 60188. All rights reserved.

Scripture quotations marked NKJV are taken from the New King James Version,® copyright © 1982 by Thomas Nelson, Inc. Used by permission. All rights reserved.

Scripture quotations marked NASB are taken from the New American Standard Bible,® copyright © 1960, 1962, 1963, 1968, 1971, 1972, 1973, 1975, 1977 by The Lockman Foundation. Used by permission.

Scripture quotations marked RSV are taken from the Revised Standard Version of the Bible, copyright © 1946, 1952, and 1971 by the National Council of the Churches of Christ in the United States of America. Used by permission. All rights reserved worldwide.

Scripture quotations marked ESV are taken from the ESV® Bible (The Holy Bible, English Standard Version®), copyright © 2001 by Crossway, a publishing ministry of Good News Publishers. Used by permission. All rights reserved.

For information about special discounts for bulk purchases, please contact Tyndale House Publishers at csresponse@tyndale.com, or call 1-800-323-9400.

Library of Congress Cataloging-in-Publication Data

Alcorn, Randy C.
   50 days of heaven : reflections that bring eternity to light / Randy Alcorn.
     p. cm.
   Includes bibliographical references.
   ISBN 978-1-4143-0976-7 (hc : alk. paper)
   1. Heaven—Christianity—Meditations. I. Title.
   BT846.3.A432 2006
   236'.24—dc22   2006009496

ISBN 978-1-4964-9106-0 LeatherLike

Printed in China

31 30 29 28 27 26 25
 8   7   6   5   4   3   2

*To Nanci Noren Alcorn,
my soulmate and treasured companion:
Heaven is richer with you there, beloved,
and Earth is poorer.
I miss you more than I can say.
But every day brings us nearer our reunion.
I look forward to amazing and delightful adventures
together forever with our King Jesus
as you and I explore that redeemed country
we were made for and so often spoke of
in our fifty-four years together in the Shadowlands:
the New Heavens and New Earth,
where there will be
no more sin,
no more death,
no more suffering,
no more curse;
the ever-unfolding story where every chapter
will be better than the one before
and where we truly will live happily ever after.
Not a fairy tale; rather,
the irrevocable blood-bought
promise of Jesus, Lamb of God and Lion of Judah,
Emmanuel: God with us, forever
and we with him
and with each other;
where we will never again have to say goodbye.*

ACKNOWLEDGMENTS

Special thanks to our friend Doreen Button, who went through every page and suggested revisions at three stages in this project. Doreen, you're a gem.

Bonnie Hiestand typed in my handwritten corrections from hard copy. Kathy Norquist, Linda Jeffries, Janet Albers, Sharon Misenhimer, and Sarah Ballenger all assisted in various ways. I'm so grateful for these sisters and all who serve so faithfully in our office at EPM.

At Tyndale House, I'm indebted to my friend and editor Dave Lindstedt and to Carol Traver, Maria Eriksen, and Ron Beers. Travis Thrasher probably did something helpful, too, though I'm not sure what. Thanks to Lynn Vanderzalm for her editorial work on earlier versions of some of the material. Thanks also to the Tyndale sales team, to Paul Mathews for his attention to the details when it comes to stewarding my books, and to all the rest at Tyndale.

Thanks to Ruthanna Metzgar for sharing her story and to my friends Steve Keels and Stu Weber for their weekly encouragement.

Thanks always and in all things to my family: Nanci, my awesome wife; our terrific sons and daughters, Dan and Angela Stump, and Dan and Karina Franklin; and our precious grandsons, Jake, Matthew, Ty, and Jack.

PREFACE
About This Book

Fifty Days of Heaven is drawn from selected portions of my larger book called *Heaven*. I've revised and refashioned segments of that book into fifty short, self-contained meditations suitable for fifty consecutive days of reflection or for reading at any pace or in any order you might choose.

I've received many encouraging responses to *Heaven*, indicating a tremendous interest in this subject matter and a desire to see it addressed in other formats. I hope this devotional will prove useful and enlightening.

This book is intended for two kinds of readers: those who haven't read *Heaven* and are drawn to something shorter than the full-length treatment and in a more devotional format; and those who have read *Heaven* but would like to come back to the subject and reflect on brief segments that are easier to absorb. I think readers of *Heaven* will agree that these shorter pieces have a very different feel and effect.

In developing these meditations, I've integrated some new material. Each day's reading includes its own introduction and conclusion, a selected passage of Scripture, and a great quote about Heaven that corresponds to the subject of the day. I've completed each meditation with a final question to ponder—often something that asks for a response—and a personal prayer that flows from the reflection.

I have chosen to capitalize the words *Heaven* and *Hell* to underscore the fact that these are real places. In other words, I am treating the names of these eternal destinations as we do any other place, such as Chicago, Nigeria, Europe, or Saturn. I also capitalize *New Earth*, for the same reason we capitalize *New England*. The only exceptions are when I am quoting writers who don't capitalize these words or when I am quoting Scripture, because none of the modern Bible translations capitalize *heaven* or *hell*.

It wasn't easy to select only fifty snapshots of Heaven for these meditations. There's so much more to be said! Nevertheless, I trust that these daily readings will help ignite your passion for Heaven, inspire you to draw closer to God, and whet your appetite to learn more about God's plan for the New Earth. If, when you're done, you want a more detailed exploration of this fascinating subject and the many Bible passages that speak of God's eternal plan, you may wish to consult the larger book, *Heaven*.

Eternal Perspective Ministries Contact Information:
Web site: www.epm.org
E-mail: info@epm.org
Phone: 503-668-5200
Mail: 39085 Pioneer Blvd., Suite 206, Sandy, OR 97055

Follow Randy Alcorn online:
www.epm.org/blog
www.facebook.com/randyalcorn
www.twitter.com/randyalcorn

INTRODUCTION
Learning to See in the Country of the Blind

[Anna] gave thanks to God and spoke about the child
to all who were looking forward to the redemption of
Jerusalem.   — LUKE 2:38

*The kingdom of God ... does not mean merely the salvation
of certain individuals nor even the salvation of a chosen group
of people. It means nothing less than the complete renewal of
the entire cosmos, culminating in the new heaven and the new
earth.*[1]   — ANTHONY HOEKEMA

Most cultures believe in an afterlife. At question is not whether people will live forever, but where they will live and in what condition. Most cultures also have a concept of Heaven and Hell. They see some people as having a quality of eternal life that is far more than mere existence and others as existing forever in a state of eternal death rather than life. This view is certainly consistent with what Jesus taught: "Then they [the unrighteous] will go away to eternal punishment, but the righteous to eternal life" (Matthew 25:46).

Sadly, many who believe in Heaven think of it as a dull and undesirable place. This perspective might best be summarized by the Irish playwright George Bernard Shaw, who observed, "Heaven, as conventionally conceived, is a place so inane, so dull, so useless, so miserable, that nobody has ever ventured to describe a whole day in heaven, though plenty of people have described a day at the seashore." Shaw's view, however, is in stark contrast to the mind-set of the early Christians, whose anticipation of Heaven we find preserved in the Roman catacombs, where the bodies of many martyred Christians of the first century were buried. These underground caverns are filled with inscriptions such as the following, found on three separate tombs:

> In Christ, Alexander is not dead, but lives.
> One who lives with God.
> He was taken up into his eternal home.

One historian writes, "Pictures on the catacomb walls portray Heaven with beautiful landscapes, children playing, and people feasting at banquets."[2]

In AD 125, a Greek named Aristides wrote to a friend about Christianity, explaining why this "new religion" was so successful: "If any righteous man among the Christians passes from this world, they rejoice and offer thanks to God, and they escort his body with songs and thanksgiving as if he were setting out from one place to another nearby."

This early Christian perspective sounds almost foreign to us today, doesn't it? But their beliefs were rooted in Scriptures such as Philippians 1:21-23, where the apostle Paul writes, "To me, to live is Christ and to die is gain. . . . Yet what shall I choose?. . . I desire to depart and be with Christ, which is better by far." Paul also writes, "As long as we are at home in the body we are away from the Lord. We . . . would prefer to be away from the body and at home with the Lord" (2 Corinthians 5:6-8).

Throughout the ages, Heaven has played a dominant role in the thoughts and lives of God's people. Heaven is the North Star by which countless Christians have navigated their lives. But have you noticed? Heaven today has largely fallen off our radar screens. If we are honest, we must admit that we are not daily and consciously looking forward to Heaven, much less to a New Earth. We've reduced Heaven to an otherworldly state, and we've ignored the clear biblical promise of a redeemed universe over which we will serve as God's delegated rulers. We've become blinded to the truth, and we've lost our vocabulary of wonder and our anticipation of the great and glorious plan that God has in store for us. Jesus said of the devil, "When he lies, he speaks his native language, for he is a liar and the father of lies" (John 8:44). Some of Satan's favorite lies are about Heaven.

In his short story "The Country of the Blind," H. G. Wells writes of a tribe in a remote valley deep in a towering mountain range, cut off from the rest of the world by a massive avalanche that has destroyed the mountain passes. As a result of a terrible epidemic, successive generations of this tribe are all born blind. Eventually, as a culture, they lose the very concept of *vision* and have no awareness of the world they're unable to see. Because of their handicap, they do not know their true condition. When an outsider, who can see, stumbles into their village, they think he is a newly formed creature, with imperfect senses, and that all his talk of seeing is craziness. They cannot understand this other dimension called *sight*. Although they have adapted themselves to their circumstances, they cannot imagine what realms might lie beyond their valley.

Spiritually speaking, we live in the Country of the Blind. The disease of sin has blinded us to the truth about God and Heaven, both of which are real, yet unseen. Fortunately, Jesus has come to our valley from Heaven to tell us about his Father and the world beyond. If we will listen to him—which requires a concerted effort to overcome our presuppositions, our ignorance, and the devil's lies—we will gain a new understanding of our present circumstances and of the world to come. We will no longer be conformed to the pattern of this world but will be transformed by the renewing of our minds (Romans 12:2). Consequently, our lives will be forever changed.

When Jesus told his disciples, "In my Father's house are many rooms. . . . I am going there to prepare a place for you" (John 14:2), he deliberately chose common, physical terms (*house*, *rooms*, *place*) to describe where he was going and what he was preparing. He wanted to give his disciples (and us) something tangible to look forward to—an actual place, a *home*, where they (and we) would go to be with him.

The Heaven that Jesus described is not an ethereal realm of disembodied spirits. Such a place could never be home for us, because human beings are not suited for a nonmaterial existence. A *place* is by nature physical, just as human beings are by nature physical as well as spiritual. What we are suited for—what we've been specifically designed for—is a place like the one that God made for us: Earth. We were made *from* the earth and *for* the earth. Earth is our home.

When Anna saw the young Jesus, "she gave thanks to God and spoke about the child to all who were looking forward to the redemption of Jerusalem" (Luke 2:36-38).

The people to whom Anna spoke about Jesus the Messiah-King, those "looking forward to the redemption of Jerusalem," were doing exactly what Peter says we should be doing: "looking forward to a new heaven and a new earth, the home of righteousness" (2 Peter 3:13). This is the gospel of the Kingdom. Anything less is a narrow and truncated concept of God's redemptive plan.

God didn't make a mistake when he formed the first human being from the dust of the earth. He wasn't speaking merely metaphorically when he said he wanted humanity to live on the earth and rule the earth. And God has not abandoned his original design and plan. One day, he will restore that which has been corrupted by sin, and he will bring Heaven down to a place called the New Earth. That is where he invites each of us to come live with him forever.

If we grasp this remarkable truth, we will realize at last that our most basic problem is not that we want *too much*. On the contrary, it is that we are content with *too little*. C. S. Lewis put it this way: "If we consider the unblushing promises of rewards in the Gospels, it would seem that our Lord finds our desires not too strong, but too weak. We are half-hearted creatures, fooling about with drink and sex and ambition when infinite joy is offered us, like an ignorant child who wants to go on making mud pies in a slum because he cannot imagine what is meant by the offer of a holiday at the sea. We are far too easily pleased."³

When it comes to understanding Heaven, have you been content with too little?

DAY 1

IF WE CAN JUST SEE THE SHORE

Rejoice that your names are written in heaven.
— Luke 10:20

It becomes us to spend this life only as a journey toward heaven.... Why should we labor for or set our hearts on anything else, but that which is our proper end and true happiness?[4]
— Jonathan Edwards

Life in this world—the way it is now and the way *we* are now—isn't easy, is it?

Perhaps you're burdened, discouraged, depressed, or even traumatized. Perhaps you've lost a loved one. Perhaps your dreams—your family, career, or lifelong ambitions—have crumbled. Perhaps you've become cynical or have lost hope. A biblical understanding of the truth about Heaven can change all that.

Secular optimists are merely wishful thinkers. Having discovered the present payoffs of optimism, they conduct seminars and write books about positive thinking. Sometimes they capitalize on optimism by becoming rich and famous. But then what happens? They eventually get old or sick, and when they die, they are unprepared to meet God. Their optimism is ultimately an illusion, for it fails to take eternity into account.

The only proper foundation for optimism is the redemptive work of Jesus Christ. If we build our lives on this solid foundation, we should all be optimists. Why? Because even our most painful experiences in life are but temporary setbacks. Our pain and suffering may or may not be relieved in this life, but they will *certainly* be relieved in the life to come. That is Christ's promise—no more pain or death; he will wipe away all our tears. He took our sufferings on himself so that one day he might remove all suffering from the world. That is the biblical foundation for our optimism. Any other foundation is like sand, not rock. It will not bear the weight of our eternity.

No Christian should be pessimistic. We should be true realists—focused on the *reality* that we serve a sovereign and gracious God. Because of the *reality* of Christ's atoning sacrifice and his promises, biblical realism *is* optimism.

By meditating on Heaven and learning to look forward to it, we don't eliminate our pain, but we can alleviate it and put it in perspective. We're reminded that suffering and death are only temporary conditions.

Jesus came to deliver us from the fear of death, "so that by his death he might destroy him who holds the power of death—that is, the devil—and free those who all their lives were held in slavery by their fear of death" (Hebrews 2:14-15).

In light of the coming resurrection of the dead, the apostle Paul asks, "Where, O death, is your victory? Where, O death, is your sting?" (1 Corinthians 15:55).

We should not romanticize death. But those who know Jesus should realize that death is a gateway to never-ending joy.

Grasping what the Bible teaches about Heaven will shift our center of gravity and radically alter our perspective on life. It will give us *hope*, a word that the apostle Paul uses six times in Romans 8:20-25, where he explains that all creation longs for our resurrection and the world's coming redemption.

Don't place your hope in favorable life circumstances—they cannot and will not last. Instead, place your hope in Jesus Christ and his promises. One day he will return, and those who have placed their faith in him will be resurrected to life on the New Earth. They will behold God's face and joyfully serve him forever.

In 1952, Florence Chadwick stepped into the waters of the Pacific Ocean off Catalina Island, California, determined to swim to the mainland. An experienced swimmer, she had already been the first woman to swim the English Channel both ways.

The weather that day was foggy and chilly; Florence could hardly see the boats accompanying her. Still, she swam steadily for fifteen hours. When she begged to be taken out of the water along the way, her mother, in a boat alongside, told her that she was close and that she could make it. Finally, physically and emotionally exhausted, Florence stopped swimming and was pulled out. It wasn't until she was aboard the boat that she discovered the shore was less than half a mile away. At a news conference the next day, she said, "All I could see was the fog. . . . I think if I could have seen the shore, I would have made it."[5]

As you face discouragement, difficulty, or fatigue, or as you are surrounded by the fog of uncertain circumstances, are you thinking, *If only I could see the shore, I could make it*?

Set your sights on Jesus Christ, the Rock of salvation. He is the one who has promised to prepare a place for those who put their hope in him, a place where they will live with him forever. If we can learn to fix our eyes on Jesus, to see through the fog and picture our eternal home in our mind's eye, it will comfort and energize us, giving us a clear look at the finish line.

When the apostle Paul faced hardship, beatings, and imprisonment, he said, "One thing I do: Forgetting what is behind and straining toward what is ahead, I press on toward the goal to win the prize for which God has called me heavenward in Christ Jesus" (Philippians 3:13-14).

What gave Paul the strength and perspective to "press on toward the goal"? A clear view of Heaven. He wanted to "win the prize" that awaited him in Heaven, and he knew that God had "called [him] heavenward in Christ Jesus."

If you're weary and don't know how you can keep going, I pray this book will give you encouragement, vision, and hope. No matter how tough life becomes, if you can see the shore and draw your strength from Christ, you'll make it.

Are you able to see the shore? Will you ask God now to help you see it?

> ☨ *O God, Father of all promise and hope, maker of a world that was once perfect and one day will be perfect again, help us to look beyond the fog of this world. Help us to see the shore of the homeland that awaits us—a glorious, eternal Kingdom purchased by the loving sacrifice of Jesus Christ, our Savior and the King of kings.*

DAY 2

HEAVENLY MINDED AND OF EARTHLY GOOD

Set your hearts on things above, where Christ is seated at the right hand of God. Set your minds on things above, not on earthly things. — Colossians 3:1-2

It is since Christians have largely ceased to think of the other world that they have become so ineffective in this.[6]
— C. S. Lewis

Over the years, a number of people have told me, "We shouldn't think about Heaven. We should just think about Jesus."

This viewpoint sounds spiritual, doesn't it? But it is based on wrong assumptions, and it is clearly contradicted by Scripture.

Colossians 3:1-2 is a direct command to set our hearts and minds on Heaven. We set our minds on Heaven because we love Jesus Christ, and Heaven is where he now resides. To long for Heaven is to long for Christ. To long for Christ is to long for

Heaven, for that is where we will be with him. That's why God's people are "longing for a better country" (Hebrews 11:16).

In Colossians 3:1, the Greek word translated "set your hearts on" is *zeteo*, which "denotes man's general philosophical search or quest."[7] The same word is used in the Gospels to describe how "the Son of Man came to *seek* and to save what was lost" (Luke 19:10, emphasis added). *Zeteo* is also used to describe how a shepherd looks for his lost sheep (Matthew 18:12), a woman searches for a lost coin (Luke 15:8), and a merchant searches for fine pearls (Matthew 13:45). It is a diligent, active, single-minded pursuit. Thus, we can understand Paul's admonition in Colossians 3:1 as follows: "Diligently, actively, single-mindedly pursue the things above"—in a word, *Heaven*.

The verb *zeteo* is in the present tense, suggesting an ongoing process. "Keep seeking Heaven." Don't just have a conversation, read a book, or listen to a sermon and feel as if you've fulfilled the command. If you're going to spend the next lifetime living in Heaven, why not spend this lifetime seeking Heaven so you can eagerly anticipate and prepare for it?

The command, and its restatement, implies there is nothing automatic about setting our minds on Heaven. In fact, most commands assume a resistance to obeying them, which sets up the necessity for the command. We are told to avoid sexual immorality because it is our tendency. We are not told to avoid jumping off buildings because normally we don't battle such a temptation. Every day, the command to think about Heaven is under attack in a hundred different ways. Everything militates against thinking about Heaven. Our minds are set so resolutely on Earth that we are unaccustomed to heavenly thinking. So we must work at it.

What have you been doing daily to set your mind on things above, to *seek* Heaven? What should you do differently?

Perhaps you're afraid of becoming "so heavenly minded that you're of no earthly good." Relax—you have nothing to worry about! On the contrary, many of us are so earthly minded we are of no heavenly *or* earthly good. As C. S. Lewis observed,

> If you read history you will find that the Christians who did most for the present world were just those who thought most of the next. The Apostles themselves, who set on foot the conversion of the Roman Empire, the great men who built up the Middle Ages, the English Evangelicals who abolished the Slave Trade, all left their mark on Earth, precisely because their minds were occupied with Heaven. It is since Christians have largely ceased to think of the other world that they have become so ineffective in this. Aim at Heaven and you will get earth "thrown in": aim at earth and you will get neither.[8]

We need a generation of heavenly minded people who see human beings and the earth itself not simply as they are, but as God intends them to be. Such people will pass on a heritage to their children far more valuable than any inheritance.

We must begin by reasoning from God's revealed truth. But such reasoning will require us to use our Scripture-enhanced imaginations. As a nonfiction writer and Bible teacher, I start by seeing what Scripture actually says. As a novelist, I take that revelation and add to it the vital ingredient of imagination.

In the words of Francis Schaeffer, "The Christian is the really free man—he is free to have imagination. This too is our heritage. The Christian is the one whose imagination should fly beyond the stars."[9]

Schaeffer always started with God's revealed truth. But he exhorted us to let that truth fuel our imagination. Imagination should not fly *away* from the truth but *upon* it.

You may be dealing with great pain and loss, yet Jesus says, "Be of good cheer" (John 16:33, NKJV). Why? Because the new house is nearly ready for you. Moving day is coming. The dark winter is about to be magically transformed into spring. One day soon you will be home—for the first time.

Until then, I encourage you to find joy and hope as you meditate on the truth about Heaven revealed in the Bible.

Why not ask God to make your imagination soar and your heart rejoice?

Thank you, God, for the gift of imagination. In a world where ideas are so often grounded in quicksand and are contrary to sound doctrine, help us to be firmly based in your Word. Help us to be saturated in its teaching. Thank you for promising us "immeasurably more than all we ask or imagine"[10] in your eternal Kingdom.

DAY 3

SEEING GOD'S FACE

[God's servants] will see his face.   — Revelation 22:4

I shall rise from the dead. . . . I shall see the Son of God, the Sun of Glory, and shine myself as that sun shines. I shall be united to the Ancient of Days, to God Himself, who had no morning, never began. . . . No man ever saw God and lived. And yet, I shall not live till I see God; and when I have seen him, I shall never die.[11]   — John Donne

Our longing for Heaven is a longing for God—a longing that involves not only our inner selves but our bodies as well. Being with God is the heart and soul of Heaven. Every other heavenly pleasure will derive from and be secondary to his holy presence. God's greatest gift to us is, and always will be, *himself*. His presence brings satisfaction. His absence brings thirst and longing.

"As the deer pants for streams of water, so my soul pants for you, O God. My soul thirsts for God, for the living God. When can I go and meet with God?" (Psalm 42:1-2).

"O God, you are my God, earnestly I seek you; my soul thirsts for you, my body longs for you, in a dry and weary land where there is no water" (Psalm 63:1).

Ancient theologians often spoke of the "beatific vision." The term comes from three Latin words that together mean "a happy-making sight." The sight they spoke of was God. To see God's face is the loftiest of all aspirations. It's sad, then, that for most of us, it's not at the top of our list of desires.

When Moses said to God, "Show me your glory," God responded, "I will cause all my goodness to pass in front of you.... [But] you cannot see my face, for no one may see me and live.... When my glory passes by, I will put you in a cleft in the rock and cover you with my hand until I have passed by. Then I will remove my hand and you will see my back; but my face must not be seen" (Exodus 33:18-23).

Moses saw God, but not God's face. The New Testament says that God "lives in unapproachable light, whom no one has seen or can see" (1 Timothy 6:16). Thus, when we're told in Revelation 22:4 that we'll see God's face, it should astound us.

"Without holiness no one will see the Lord" (Hebrews 12:14). The obstacles to seeing God are daunting. It's only because we'll be fully righteous in Christ and completely sinless that we'll be able to see God and live. To see God will be our greatest joy, the joy by which all other joys will be measured.

David says, "One thing I ask of the LORD, this is what I seek: that I may dwell in the house of the LORD all the days of my life, to gaze upon the beauty of the LORD and to seek him in his temple" (Psalm 27:4). David was preoccupied with God's person, and also with God's place. He longed to be where God was and to gaze on his beauty. To see God's face is to behold his beauty.

When Jesus Christ came to Earth as one of us (John 1:14), God, who is transcendent, became immanent. Thus, one of the names given to Jesus is Immanuel, "God with us" (Matthew 1:23). Because God the Father and God the Son are one (John 10:30), whenever we see Jesus in Heaven, we will see *God*. Because Jesus Christ is a permanent manifestation of God, he could say to his disciple Philip, "Anyone who has seen me has seen the Father" (John 14:9). Certainly, then, a primary way that we will see God the Father on the New Earth is through his Son, Jesus.

Jesus also says, "Blessed are the pure in heart, for they will see God" (Matthew 5:8). In Revelation 22:4, when it says "they will see his face, and his name will be on their foreheads," it appears to be referring to seeing the face of God the Father.

Does God, who is not inherently physical, have a face in any sense but a figurative one? I'm not certain. And I don't pretend to understand how we will see his face. But I rejoice in the anticipation that we will!

Scripture is full of great promises about what awaits us in Heaven. However, none is greater than the promise that we, as resurrected human beings, will actually *see* God.

If you're a follower of Jesus, what would you like to say now to the God whom you will one day see?

Father, fill us with the wonder of being able to see you face-to-face, to walk beside your Son and behold his eternally human and divine face. What a delight to gaze at you, the source of all good, all beauty, all mystery. And what an incomparable experience to not only imagine but one day actually see your face—you who spun the galaxies into existence, who wove together the earth with its animals and oceans and forests and flowers, who created us in your glorious image. May we never lose sight of our highest destiny, to see you. And may we pass on that vision to those around us, including our children and grandchildren.

DAY 4

GOD: OUR PRIMARY PLEASURE

I know that my Redeemer lives, and that in the end he will stand upon the earth. And after my skin has been destroyed, yet in my flesh I will see God; I myself will see him with my own eyes. — JOB 19:25-27

The redeemed will indeed enjoy other things. . . . But that which they shall enjoy in the angels, or each other, or in anything else whatsoever, that will yield them delight and happiness, will be what will be seen of God in them.[12]
— JONATHAN EDWARDS

The anticipation of seeing God face-to-face is heartfelt and ancient. In the oldest recorded book of Scripture—most likely written before Moses wrote Genesis—Job, in the midst of bone-crushing anguish, cried out in a vision of striking clarity that his Redeemer would one day come to Earth. And even though Job's body would be destroyed through physical death, he knew that he would in his own flesh see God. It's hard to imagine a clearer reference to the coming resurrection.

In what form will we be when we see God? Will we be ghostly

spirits, floating about? No, we will be resurrected human beings, standing and kneeling, walking and talking, praying and worshiping and laughing, eating and drinking *in our new bodies*. As Job cried out, "After my skin has been destroyed, yet in my flesh I will see God."

When Job imagined seeing his Redeemer with his own eyes, it flooded his troubled soul with a transcendent sense of victory and comfort. As you anticipate seeing God face-to-face, what images come to mind? What effect do those images have on you?

Will the Christ we worship in Heaven as God also be human? Yes. According to Hebrews 13:8, "Jesus Christ is the same yesterday [when he lived on Earth] and today [when he lives in the present Heaven] and forever [when he will live on the New Earth, in the eternal Heaven]."

Jesus didn't put on a body and then shed it again as if it were a coat. He doesn't comprise two separable components, man and God, to be switched on and off. He was and is and always will be God *and* a man. The Incarnation is permanent.

We need not wait until the New Earth to catch glimpses of God. We're told his "invisible qualities" can be "clearly seen" in "what has been made" (Romans 1:20). Yes, we live amid devastation, and we know the corruption of our own hearts. Yes, our vision is hampered by the curse that affects all of creation. Eden has been trampled, torched, and savaged. Nevertheless, the stars in the sky declare God's glory (Psalm 19:1); in our own bodies we can see the intricacy of God's craftsmanship; and in flowers and rain and art and music we see vestiges of God's beauty and creativity. And one day the Curse will be reversed. One day, both we and the universe will be forever set free. In that day, *we will see God*.

In Heaven, the barriers between redeemed human beings and God will be removed forever. We will look into God's eyes and see what we've always longed to see: the person who made us for his own good pleasure. Seeing God will be like seeing everything else for the first time. Why? Because not only will we see God, he will be the lens through which we see everything else—other people, ourselves, and the events of our earthly lives.

Jonathan Edwards said, "The redeemed will indeed enjoy other things. . . . But that which they shall enjoy in the angels, or each other, or in anything else whatsoever, that will yield them delight and happiness, will be what will be seen of God in them."[13]

In Psalm 73:25, Asaph says, "Whom have I in heaven but you? And earth has nothing I desire besides you." This may seem an overstatement—there's *nothing* on Earth this man desires but God? But Asaph is affirming that the central desire of our hearts is for God. Yes, we desire many other things—but in desiring them, it is really *God* we desire.

Augustine called God "the end of our desires." He prayed, "You have made us for yourself, O Lord, and our hearts are restless until they rest in you."[14]

God is the Fountainhead, the Source of all lesser streams of our desire. When we desire food, friendship, work, play, music, drama, or art, we are ultimately *desiring God*.

Consider this analogy: When you're sick and your friend brings you a meal, what meets your needs—the meal or the friend? *Both*. Without your friend, there would be no meal; but even without the meal, you would still treasure your friendship. Thus, your friend is both your higher pleasure *and* the source of your secondary pleasure (the meal). Likewise, God is the source of all lesser goods, so that when they satisfy us, it is God himself who is satisfying us.

Perhaps you're thinking, *But our eyes should be on the giver, not the gift* and, thus, *We ought to focus on God, not on Heaven*. But this perspective erroneously divorces our experience of God from life, relationships, and the world—all of which God graciously gives us to draw us closer to him. It also sees the material realm and other people as God's competitors rather than as instruments that communicate his love and character. It fails to recognize that because God is the ultimate source of joy, and all secondary joys derive from him, to love secondary joys on this earth *can be*—and in Heaven *always will be*—to love God, their source.

Do you want to ask God to help you learn to see him as the source of every good thing and thus as the one you most desire?

> *Father, given the current darkness around us, and the spiritual battles within us, we need your help to avoid making idols of your provisions. Help us realize that once you have forever freed us from sin, once we live in your presence and see your face, we'll never have to worry about putting people or things above you. That would be unthinkable. And if we were thinking clearly now, it would be unthinkable to us already. So empower us to think clearly, Lord. May we see you as you are, so we may always enjoy but never idolize the magnificent lesser desires and joys you have graciously granted to us. Use the things that delight us to draw us closer to you.*

DAY 5

ENJOYING GOD IN SECONDARY PLEASURES

He who did not spare his own Son, but gave him up for us all—how will he not also, along with him, graciously give us all things? — ROMANS 8:32

God himself, who is the Author of virtue, shall be our reward. As there is nothing greater or better than God himself, God has promised us himself. God shall be the end of all our desires, who will be seen without end, loved without cloy, and praised without weariness.[15] — AUGUSTINE

Do you think God is pleased when we enjoy a good meal, a football game, laughter with friends, a cozy fire, or a good book? Your answer to that question not only demonstrates your view of God but also indicates the degree to which you are able to enjoy life. And it will determine how much you will look forward to the resurrection and what the Bible calls the New Earth.

Scripture says, "Command those who are rich in this present world not to be arrogant nor to put their hope in wealth, which is so uncertain, but to put their hope in God, who richly provides us with everything for our enjoyment" (1 Timothy 6:17). God, not wealth, should be the object of our hope. But God is also the one who richly grants us his provisions, which are intended for our *enjoyment*.

Failure to understand the goodness of God's creation has blinded countless people from seeing Heaven as a place of great pleasure and enjoyment. Instead, they think that for Heaven to be "spiritual," it must somehow be drab, unappealing, and bereft of "earthly" things, which they consider unspiritual.

God's first commandment is that we should put no created thing before him. We should never make what he has created into a God substitute. But sometimes we wrongly conclude that people and things and pleasures are therefore bad, forgetting that it was God himself who made them.

God is not up in Heaven frowning at us and saying, "Stop it—you should find joy only in me." This would be as foreign to our heavenly Father's nature as it would be to mine as an earthly father if I gave my daughters a Christmas gift and then pouted because they enjoyed it too much. No, I gave the gift to bring joy to them and to me. I am *delighted* when they enjoy the gifts I've given them. If they didn't, I'd be disappointed. Their pleasure in my gift to them draws them closer to me.

Though preoccupation with a God-given gift can turn into idolatry, enjoying that same gift with a grateful heart can draw us closer to God. In Heaven, we'll have no capacity to turn people or things into idols. When we find joy in God's gifts, we'll find our joy in him. Enjoying God's gifts to us should never move us away from him; it should always draw us closer.

All secondary joys are *derivative* in nature. They cannot be separated from our primary joy, which is God. Flowers are beautiful because God is beautiful. Rainbows are stunning because God is stunning. Puppies are delightful because God is delightful. Sports are fun because God is fun. Study is rewarding because God is rewarding. Work is fulfilling because God is fulfilling.

Ironically, sometimes people who are the most determined to avoid the sacrilege of putting things before God miss a thousand daily opportunities to thank him, praise him, and draw near to him because they imagine they shouldn't enjoy the very things that God has made to help us know him and love him.

God is a lavish giver. "He who did not spare his own Son, but gave him up for us all—how will he not also, along with him, graciously give us all things?" (Romans 8:32). The God who gave us his Son delights to graciously give us "all things." These "things" are in addition to Christ, but they are never *instead* of him—they come "along with him." If we didn't have Christ, we would have nothing. But because we have Christ, we have everything. Hence, we can enjoy the people and things that God has made, and in the process we enjoy the God who designed and provided them for his own pleasure and ours.

God welcomes prayers of thanksgiving for meals, warm fires, games, books, hobbies, sex, and every other good thing. When we fail to acknowledge God as the source of all good things, we fail to give him the recognition and glory he deserves. We separate God from joy, which is like trying to separate heat from fire or wetness from rain.

The movie *Babette's Feast* depicts a conservative Christian sect that renounces "worldly" distractions—until Babette prepares an unforgettable dinner that opens their eyes to the richness of

God's provision. When we partake in heartfelt gratitude to God, these things draw us *closer* to God, not away from him. That's precisely what all things and all beings in Heaven will do—draw us to God.

In our lives on Earth, we should see God everywhere in his creation: in the food we eat, the friendships we enjoy, and the pleasures of family, work, and hobbies. But we should never let these secondary pleasures eclipse our love for God (and thus we, in fact, must sometimes forgo them). We should thank him for all of life's joys, large and small, and allow them to draw us closer to him.

That's exactly what we'll do in Heaven. Why not start now?

Father, many of us have lost sight of the fact that you created the earth and that you are the inventor of pleasure. You created our bodies with nerve endings and taste buds and senses that allow us to find pleasure. But as a result of the Fall, we've misused your gracious provisions and turned them into idols. We've made substitute gods out of sex and money and food and a thousand other good things. Lord, only when we understand how you have richly provided the material world for our enjoyment can we then embrace your plan to reclaim what has been lost. Help us to see that pleasure is not unspiritual, that it is from your hand and for our enjoyment within the bounds of your commandments, which are designed to keep us from destruction. Help us to pursue you as the Great Pleasure from which every lesser pleasure flows.

DAY 6

KNOWING FOR SURE THAT WE'RE GOING TO HEAVEN

Nothing impure will ever enter [the New Jerusalem, on the New Earth], nor will anyone who does what is shameful or deceitful, but only those whose names are written in the Lamb's book of life. — REVELATION 21:27

I have met no people who fully disbelieved in Hell and also had a living and life-giving belief in Heaven.[16]
— C. S. LEWIS

For every American who believes he's going to Hell, there are 120 who believe they're going to Heaven.[17] This optimism stands in stark contrast to Christ's words in Matthew 7:13-14: "Enter through the narrow gate. For wide is the gate and broad is the road that leads to destruction, and many enter through it. But small is the gate and narrow the road that leads to life, and only a few find it."

We tend to assume that we are automatically going to Heaven, but we overlook the fact that our sin is sufficient to keep us out: "All have sinned and fall short of the glory of God" (Romans

3:23). Sin separates us from a relationship with God (Isaiah 59:2). "Your eyes are too pure to look on evil; you cannot tolerate wrong" (Habakkuk 1:13). Because we are sinners, we are not entitled to enter God's presence. Because we cannot enter Heaven as we are, Heaven is *not* our default destination. Before we can see God in Heaven, something must radically change—because, unless our sin problem is resolved, the only place we will go is to our true default destination: Hell.

I am addressing this issue now because throughout this book we will talk about being with Jesus, being reunited with family and friends, and enjoying great adventures in Heaven. The great danger is that readers will *assume* they are headed for Heaven. Judging by what's said at most funerals, you'd think nearly everyone's going to Heaven. But Jesus, in Matthew 7, made it clear that most people are *not*.

In the Bible, Jesus says more about Hell than anyone else does (Matthew 10:28; 13:40-42; Mark 9:43). He refers to it as a literal place and describes it in graphic terms—including raging fires and the worm that doesn't die. He says the unsaved "will be thrown outside, into the darkness, where there will be weeping and gnashing of teeth" (Matthew 8:12). In the story of the rich man and Lazarus, Jesus taught that in Hell the wicked suffer terribly, are fully conscious, retain their desires and memories and reasoning, long for relief, cannot be comforted, cannot leave their torment, and are bereft of hope (Luke 16:19-31). He could not have painted a more bleak or graphic picture.

Revelation 21:27 says, "Nothing impure will ever enter [the New Jerusalem], nor will anyone who does what is shameful or deceitful, but only those whose names are written in the Lamb's book of life."

My friend Ruthanna Metzgar, a professional singer, tells a story that illustrates the importance of having our names written in the Book of Life. She was asked to sing at the wedding of a very wealthy man. The wedding reception was to be held on the top two floors of Seattle's Columbia Tower, the Northwest's tallest skyscraper. Ruthanna and her husband, Roy, were excited about attending.

At the start of the reception, the bride and groom approached a beautiful glass and brass staircase that led to the top floor. Someone ceremoniously cut a satin ribbon draped across the bottom of the stairs, and the bride and groom ascended, followed by their guests.

At the top of the stairs, outside the door to the great banquet room, the maitre d' stood holding a bound book.

"May I have your name, please?"

"I'm Ruthanna Metzgar and this is my husband, Roy."

He searched the *M*'s. "I'm not finding it. Would you spell it, please?"

Ruthanna spelled her name slowly. After searching the book, the maitre d' looked up and said, "I'm sorry, but your name isn't here."

"There must be some mistake," Ruthanna replied. "I'm the singer!"

The gentleman answered, "It doesn't matter who you are or what you did. Without your name in the book you cannot attend the banquet."

He motioned to a waiter and said, "Show these people to the service elevator, please."

The Metzgars followed the waiter past beautifully decorated tables laden with shrimp, whole smoked salmon, and magnificent carved ice sculptures. Adjacent to the banquet area, an orchestra was preparing to perform, the musicians all dressed in dazzling white tuxedos.

The waiter led Ruthanna and Roy to the service elevator, ushered them in, and pressed *G* for the parking garage.

After driving several miles in silence, Roy reached over and put his hand on Ruthanna's arm. "Sweetheart, what happened?"

"When the invitation arrived, I was busy," Ruthanna replied. "I never bothered to RSVP. Besides, I was the singer. Surely I could go to the reception without returning the RSVP!"

Ruthanna started to weep—not only because she had missed the most lavish banquet she'd ever been invited to, but also because she suddenly had a small taste of what it will be like someday for people as they stand before Christ and find that their names are not written in the Lamb's Book of Life.[18]

Throughout the ages, countless people have been too busy to respond to Christ's invitation to his wedding banquet. Many assume that the good they've done—perhaps attending church, being baptized, singing in the choir, or helping in a soup kitchen— will be enough to earn their entry to Heaven. But no explanation or excuse will count. All that will matter is whether our names are written in the book. If we haven't responded to God's invitation, we'll be turned away.

To be denied entrance to Heaven's wedding feast will not mean just going down the service elevator to the garage. It will mean being cast outside into Hell, forever.

Forgiveness is not automatic. If we want to be forgiven, we must recognize and repent of our sins: "He who conceals his sins does not prosper, but whoever confesses and renounces them finds mercy" (Proverbs 28:13). Forgiveness is established by our confession: "If we confess our sins, he is faithful and just and will forgive us our sins and purify us from all unrighteousness" (1 John 1:9). There's no righteous deed we can do that will earn us a place in Heaven (Titus 3:5). We come to Christ empty handed. We can take no credit for salvation: "For it is by grace you have been saved, through faith—and this not from yourselves, it is the gift of God—not by works, so that no one can boast" (Ephesians 2:8-9).

Jesus Christ offers everyone the gifts of forgiveness, salvation, and eternal life: "Whoever is thirsty, let him come; and whoever wishes, let him take the free gift of the water of life" (Revelation 22:17). God determined that he would rather go to Hell on our behalf than live in Heaven without us. He wants us *not* to go to Hell so much that he paid a horrible price on the cross so that we wouldn't have to.

Have you said yes to Christ's invitation to join him at the wedding feast and spend eternity with him in his house? If so, you have reason to rejoice—Heaven's gates will be open to you. But if you have been putting off your response, or if you assume that you can enter Heaven without responding to Christ's invitation, one day you will deeply regret your decision, or your indecision.

Have you said yes to God's invitation? Can you think of a better time than right now to say yes?

━✛ *God, I pray for any readers who have not yet claimed your gift of salvation through Jesus. Move their hearts to repent of their sins and to give their lives over to you. You know whose names are written in your book. Bring people to faith in Jesus so that they may be made right with you through Christ's redemptive work and so that they may spend a wonderful eternity together with you in Heaven. Lord, what a miracle that you have offered Heaven to us, who deserve Hell. Thank you for your offer of grace, which was so costly to you that it might be free to us.*

DAY 7

HEAVEN ON EARTH

Then I saw a new heaven and a new earth.... And I heard a loud voice from the throne saying, "Now the dwelling of God is with men, and he will live with them. They will be his people, and God himself will be with them and be their God." — REVELATION 21:1, 3

The "new Jerusalem"... does not remain in a "heaven" far off in space, but it comes down to the renewed earth; there the redeemed will spend eternity in resurrection bodies. So heaven and earth, now separated, will then be merged: the new earth will also be heaven, since God will dwell there with his people.[19] — ANTHONY HOEKEMA

When we speak about the coming New Earth, much of what we say about it may *not* apply to the Heaven we go to when we die. For instance, Scripture makes it clear that we will eat and drink in our resurrection bodies on the New Earth (Isaiah 25:6; Matthew 8:11; Luke 22:18, 29-30; Revelation 19:9). But that doesn't mean people eat and drink in the *present Heaven*, the place where God's people who have departed from Earth now live. Remember, those now in Heaven *do not yet have resurrection bodies*. (Theologians debate whether the saints have temporary physical forms there, but certainly our current bodies will remain in the grave until the resurrection.) Likewise, when we describe the present Heaven, it will not necessarily correspond with what the eternal Heaven—the New Earth—will be like.

Does this sound confusing? I understand. But once you abandon the assumption that Heaven cannot change, it all makes perfect sense. Think with me. *God* does not change, but God clearly says that Heaven *will* change. For one thing, it will eventually be relocated to the New Earth (Revelation 21:1-2).

Because God created Heaven, it had a beginning and thus is neither timeless nor changeless. It had a *past*—the time prior to Christ's incarnation. It has a *present*—the present or intermediate Heaven, where believers go when they die. And it will have a *future*—the eternal Heaven, or New Earth.

The past Heaven, the present Heaven, and the future Heaven can all be called Heaven because they are all God's dwelling places. Yet *they are not synonymous*. The present Heaven is in the angelic realm, distinctly separate from Earth. By contrast, the future Heaven will be in the human realm, on Earth, in a resurrected universe. Then the dwelling place of God will also be the dwelling place of humanity: "I saw a new heaven and a new earth. . . . I saw the Holy City, the new Jerusalem, coming down out of heaven from God. . . . And I heard a loud voice from the throne saying, 'Now the dwelling of God is with men, and he will live with them. They will be his people, and God himself will be with them and be their God'" (Revelation 21:1-3).

When the New Jerusalem, which *was* in Heaven, comes down out of Heaven from God, where will it go? To the New Earth. From that time on, God's dwelling place—Heaven—will be with his redeemed people, on *Earth*.

Some would argue that the New Earth shouldn't be called Heaven. But if Heaven, by definition, is God's special dwelling place and we're told that "the dwelling of God" will be with mankind on Earth, then Heaven and the New Earth must essentially be the same place. Wherever God dwells with his people and sits on his throne is Heaven. And we're clearly told that "the throne of God and of the Lamb" is in the New Jerusalem, which is brought down to the New Earth (Revelation 21:1-3; 22:1).

God, who is omnipresent, may dwell centrally wherever he wishes. Wherever he chooses to put his throne *is* Heaven. He has revealed that he will relocate his central dwelling from the place we now call Heaven to the New Earth to live with his risen people. When he puts his kingdom throne on the New Earth, it will transform the New Earth into Heaven.

Jesus says of anyone who would be his disciple, "My Father will love him, and we will come to him and make our home with him" (John 14:23). This is a picture of God's ultimate plan—not to take us up to live in a realm made for him, but to come down and live with us *in the realm he made for us*. Think about this: In God's original plan, he could have taken Adam and Eve up to Heaven to visit with him—but he didn't. Instead, he came down to walk with them in their own world (Genesis 3:8).

When Jesus Christ came to Earth, one of the names given to him was Immanuel, which means "God with us." The Incarnation means that God came down to live with us. And when Jesus ascended to Heaven in his resurrected body, it demonstrated that the Incarnation wasn't temporary, but permanent. This has great bearing on where God might choose for us and him to dwell together. The New Earth will be Heaven incarnate, just as Jesus Christ is God incarnate.

Several books on Heaven state that the New Jerusalem will not descend to Earth but will remain suspended overhead. But Revelation 21:2 doesn't say this. When John watches the city "coming down" from Heaven, there's no reason to believe it stops before reaching the New Earth. (If we said that a plane was coming down from the sky, we wouldn't assume it never landed, would we?) The assumption that the New Jerusalem remains suspended over the earth arises from the notion that Heaven and Earth must always be separate. But Scripture indicates they will be joined. Their present incompatibility is due to a temporary aberration—Earth is under sin and the Curse. Once that aberration is corrected, Heaven and Earth will be fully compatible again (Ephesians 1:10).

Utopian idealists who dream of mankind creating "Heaven on Earth" are destined for disappointment. But though they are wrong in believing that humans can achieve it, the fact is that there will be Heaven on Earth. That's *God*'s dream. It's *God*'s plan. And he—not we—will accomplish it.

Is the idea of Heaven coming down to Earth a foreign concept to you? What do you think about living on a New Earth that is also Heaven? Can you imagine anything better than that?

⇌ Father, what a great truth it is that Jesus came down to be with us in the Incarnation. And how incredible that he not only became a man but will forever be the God-man. What amazing grace you showed to us by inhabiting space and time as a human being. It's hard to imagine the eternal Son of God, the Creator of the universe, becoming a human child—carried by a Galilean peasant woman, born in a Bethlehem barn, surrounded by human blood and animals and straw, wrapped to keep out the cold night air. And how amazing, too, that you promise one day to come down and live with us again in our home, the New Earth. Millions of years from now, Father, surely we will still be awestruck with wonder at your glorious plan!

DAY 8

WHERE GOD'S PEOPLE GO WHEN THEY DIE

Brothers, we do not want you to be ignorant about those who fall asleep, or to grieve like the rest of men, who have no hope. — 1 Thessalonians 4:13

Oh, God, this is the end; but for me it is just the beginning.
— Dietrich Bonhoeffer,
just before he was hanged by the Nazis

When Marco Polo returned to Italy from the court of Kublai Khan, he described a world his audience had never seen—one that could be understood only through the eyes of imagination. Not that China was an imaginary realm, but it was very different from Italy. Yet, as two locations on planet Earth inhabited by human beings, they had much in common. The reference points of Italy allowed a basis for understanding China, and the differences could be spelled out from there.[20]

The writers of Scripture present Heaven in many ways; for instance, as a garden, a city, a country, and a kingdom. We're familiar with gardens, cities, countries, and kingdoms; they serve as mental bridges to help us understand Heaven.

Usually when we refer to Heaven, we mean the place where Christians go when they die. When we tell our children, "Grandma's now in Heaven," we're referring to the present, or intermediate, Heaven. The term *intermediate* doesn't mean it is halfway between Heaven and Hell, in some kind of purgatory or second-rate place. The intermediate Heaven is fully Heaven, fully in God's presence, but it is intermediate in the sense that it's *temporary*, not our final destination. Though it is a wonderful place, and we'll love it there, it is not the place we are ultimately made for, and it is not the place where we will live forever. God has destined his children to live as resurrected beings on a resurrected Earth.

So, as wonderful as the present Heaven is, we must not lose sight of our true destination, the New Earth, which will also be in God's presence (because that's what Heaven is, the central place of God's dwelling).

Will Christians live in Heaven forever? The answer depends on what we mean by *Heaven*. Will we be *with the Lord* forever? Absolutely. Will we always be with him in exactly the same place that Heaven is *now*? No.

In the present Heaven, everyone is in Christ's presence, and everyone is joyful. But everyone is also looking forward to Christ's return to Earth, when they will experience their resurrection and walk on the earth again.

It may seem strange to say that the Heaven we go to at death isn't eternal, but it's true. "Christians often talk about living with God 'in heaven' forever," writes Wayne Grudem, "but in fact the biblical teaching is richer than that: it tells us that there will be new heavens and a new earth—an entirely renewed creation—and we will live with God there. . . . There will also be a new kind of unification of heaven and earth. . . . There will be a joining of heaven and earth in this new creation."[21]

Let me suggest an analogy to illustrate the difference between the present Heaven and the eternal Heaven. Suppose you live in a homeless shelter in Miami. One day you inherit a beautiful house in Santa Barbara, California, fully furnished, on a gorgeous hillside overlooking the ocean. With the home comes a wonderful job doing something you've always wanted to do. Not only that, but you'll also be near close family members who moved from Miami many years ago.

On your flight to Santa Barbara, you'll change planes in Denver, where you'll spend an afternoon. Some other family members, whom you haven't seen in years, will meet you at the Denver airport and board the plane with you to Santa Barbara, where they have inherited their own beautiful houses on another part of the same vast estate. Naturally, you look forward to seeing them. Now, when the Miami ticket agent asks you, "Where are you headed?" would you say, "Denver"? No. You would say, "Santa Barbara," because that's your final destination. If you mentioned Denver at all, you would say, "I'm going to Santa Barbara *by way of* Denver."

When you talk to your friends in Miami about where you're going to live, would you focus on Denver? No. You might not even mention Denver, even though you will be a Denver-dweller for several hours. Even if you left the airport and spent a day or a week in Denver, it still wouldn't be your focus. Denver is just an intermediate stop along the way. Your true destination—your new long-term home—is in Santa Barbara.

Similarly, the Heaven we will go to when we die, the present Heaven, is a temporary dwelling place. It's a wonderfully nice place (much better than the Denver airport!), but it's still a stop along the way to our final destination: the New Earth. It will be great to see friends and family in the present Heaven whom we haven't seen for a while. But like us, they will be looking forward to the resurrection, after which we will actually live on the estate that God is preparing for us.

Another analogy is more precise but also more difficult to envision, because for most of us it's outside our experience. Imagine leaving the homeless shelter in Miami and flying to the intermediate location, Denver, and then turning around and *going back* to your city of origin, which has been completely renovated—a New Miami. In this New Miami, you would no longer live in a homeless shelter but in a beautiful house in a glorious pollution-free, crime-free, sin-free city. So you would end up living not in a new home but in *a radically improved version of your old home.*

This is what the Bible promises us—we will live with Christ and one another forever, not in the present Heaven, but on the New Earth, which God will make into Heaven by virtue of the location of his throne and his presence, and where he will forever be at home with his people.

The idea that the present Heaven is an intermediate Heaven may or may not be a brand-new concept to you, but does it make sense? (Keep reading; I think it will.)

Father, thank you that when your children die, they step into the fullness of your presence. To be with you is to be at home. Thank you also that you have promised to take us back one day to live on a glorious New Earth. And so we look forward not only to the present Heaven but also to the new Heaven and the New Earth. Thank you, dear Lord, for the joy infused into our hearts by the thought of living forever with you, the person for whom we were made, in Heaven, the place for which you made us.

DAY 9

THE PRESENT HEAVEN: A PHYSICAL PLACE?

I see heaven open and the Son of Man standing at the right hand of God. — Acts 7:56

Soon you will read in the newspaper that I am dead. Don't believe it for a moment. I will be more alive than ever before. . . . Earth recedes. . . . Heaven opens before me![22]
— D. L. Moody, on his deathbed

At death, our bodies go to the ground, while our spirits leave this world and go to another. "The dust returns to the ground it came from, and the spirit returns to God who gave it" (Ecclesiastes 12:7).

When leaving the body, the human spirit goes to either Heaven or Hell. Jesus depicted Lazarus and the rich man as conscious in Heaven and Hell immediately after they died (Luke 16:22-31). A number of other passages make it clear that there is no such thing as "soul sleep," or a long period of unconsciousness between life on Earth and life in Heaven. Jesus told the dying thief on the cross, "Today you will be with me in paradise" (Luke 23:43). The apostle Paul said that to die was to be with Christ (Philippians 1:23) and to be absent from the body was to be present with the Lord (2 Corinthians 5:8). After their deaths, martyrs are pictured in Heaven, crying out to God to bring justice on Earth (Revelation 6:9-11).

The phrase *fall asleep* (in 1 Thessalonians 4:13 and similar passages) is a euphemism for death, describing the body's outward appearance. The spirit's departure from the body ends our existence on Earth. The physical part of us "sleeps" until the resurrection, while the spiritual part of us relocates to a conscious existence in Heaven (Daniel 12:2-3; 2 Corinthians 5:8). Every reference in Revelation to human beings talking and worshiping in Heaven prior to the resurrection of the dead demonstrates that our spiritual beings are conscious, not sleeping, after death.

The present Heaven is normally invisible to those living on Earth. But this doesn't mean it isn't physical. And even if it isn't physical, that doesn't mean it isn't real. The Bible teaches that sometimes humans are allowed to see into Heaven. When Stephen was being stoned because of his faith in Christ, he "looked up to heaven and saw the glory of God, and Jesus standing at the right hand of God. 'Look,' he said, 'I see heaven open and the Son of Man standing at the right hand of God'" (Acts 7:55-56). Scripture tells us that Stephen did not dream this but actually *saw* it. God didn't create a vision for Stephen in order to make Heaven *appear* physical. Rather, he allowed Stephen to see the present Heaven, which *was* (and is) physical.

The prophet Elisha asked God to give his servant, Gehazi, a glimpse of the invisible realm. He prayed, "'O LORD, open his eyes so he may see.' Then the LORD opened the servant's eyes, and he looked and saw the hills full of horses and chariots of fire all around Elisha" (2 Kings 6:17). It could be argued that these horses and chariots (bearing angelic warriors) exist beside us in our universe, but we are normally blind to them. Or they may be in a universe next to ours that opens up into ours so that angelic beings—and horses, apparently—can move between universes.

The text is clear that Stephen and Gehazi saw things that were actual and physical. This supports the view that Heaven is a physical realm. *Physical* and *spiritual* are neither opposite nor contradictory. In fact, the apostle Paul refers to the resurrection body as a "spiritual body" (1 Corinthians 15:44). God is a spirit and angels are spirit beings, but both can—and will on the New Earth—live in a physical environment.

If a blind man momentarily gained his sight and described an actual tree that he saw, other blind people—especially if they lived in a world where everyone was blind—might automatically assume the tree was not literal. They might think the description of the tree was a mere symbol of some spiritual reality. But they would be wrong. Likewise, we should not assume that the Bible describes Heaven in physical ways merely to accommodate us.

The biblical portrayals of the present Heaven make it seem likely that it is a physical realm, at least in some sense. But whether or not it is physical, the present Heaven is certainly *real*. It is a real place we go to—a place where we will be with God and his people, a place without sin and without suffering.

Isn't that something to look forward to every day of your life?

Lord, you have made us to be people who desire a place. Thank you that at death we will go home to be with you. Thank you that there is a real place awaiting us. Thank you that the blood of Jesus provides the means for our entrance and that many of your people have gone there before us. We praise you for the wonders of your love, which we do not deserve but which we gladly and gratefully receive.

DAY 10

PARADISE: THE PRESENT HEAVEN

> Jesus answered him, "I tell you the truth, today you will be with me in paradise." — LUKE 23:43

> *Let us greet the day which assigns each of us to his own home, which snatches us from this place and sets us free from the snares of the world, and restores us to paradise and the kingdom. Anyone who has been in foreign lands longs to return to his own native land. . . . We regard paradise as our native land.*[23] — CYPRIAN

While he was hanging from the cross in agony, Jesus reassured a thief who begged him to remember him, "Today you will be with me in paradise" (Luke 23:43). Jesus was referring to the present Heaven, where both he and the thief would go after they died. But why did he call it *paradise*? In what sense is the present Heaven paradise?

The word *paradise* comes from the Persian *pairidaeza*, meaning "a walled park" or "an enclosed garden." It was used to describe the great walled gardens of the Persian king Cyrus's royal palaces. In the Greek translation of the Old Testament, the word is used to describe the Garden of Eden (Genesis 2:8; Ezekiel 28:13). Later, because of the Jewish belief that God would restore Eden, *paradise* became the word to describe the eternal state of the righteous and, to a lesser extent, the present Heaven.[24]

Paradise does not refer to wild nature but to nature under mankind's dominion. The garden or park was not left to grow entirely on its own. People brought their creativity to bear on managing, cultivating, and presenting the garden or park. According to Oxford professor Alister McGrath, "The idea of a walled garden, enclosing a carefully cultivated area of exquisite plants and animals, was the most powerful symbol of paradise available to the human imagination, mingling the images of the beauty of nature with the orderliness of human construction. . . . The whole of human history is thus enfolded in the subtle interplay of sorrow over a lost paradise, and the hope of its final restoration."[25]

Historically, paradise was not generally understood as mere allegory, with a "spiritual meaning," but as an actual physical place where God and his people lived together, surrounded by physical beauty, enjoying great pleasures and happiness.

God says, "To him who overcomes, I will give the right to eat from the tree of life, which is in the paradise of God" (Revelation 2:7). The same physical tree of life that was in the Garden of Eden will one day be in the New Jerusalem on the New Earth (Revelation 22:2). For the time being, it is (present tense) in the intermediate Heaven. Shouldn't we assume it has the same physical properties it had in the Garden of Eden and will have in the New Jerusalem? If it doesn't, could it rightly be called the tree of life?

After the Fall, God "drove the man out; and at the east of

the garden of Eden He stationed the cherubim and the flaming sword which turned every direction to guard the way to the tree of life" (Genesis 3:24, NASB). It appears that Eden's paradise, with the tree of life, retained its identity as a physical place but was no longer accessible to mankind. It was guarded by cherubim, who are residents of Heaven, where God is "enthroned between the cherubim" (2 Kings 19:15).

Eden was not destroyed. What was destroyed was mankind's ability to live in Eden. There's no indication that Eden was stripped of its physicality and transformed into a spiritual entity. It appears to have remained just as it was, a physical paradise removed to a realm we can't gain access to—most likely the present Heaven, because we know for certain that's where the tree of life now is (Revelation 2:7).

God is not done with Eden. He preserved it not as a museum piece, but as a place that mankind will one day occupy again—and to a certain extent may now occupy in the present Heaven. Because we're told that the tree of life will be located in the New Jerusalem, on both sides of a great river (Revelation 22:2), it seems likely that the original Eden may be a great park at the center of the city. If the tree that distinguished Eden will be there, why not Eden itself? This would fit perfectly with the statement in Revelation 2:7 that the tree of life is presently in paradise.

When the rest of the earth fell under human sin, Eden was for some reason treated differently. Perhaps it had come from Heaven, God's dwelling place, and was transplanted to Earth. We don't know. But we do know this: Before the Fall, God came to Eden to visit with Adam and Eve (Genesis 3:8). After the Fall, Adam and Eve were banished from the Garden, so God could no longer visit them there. Whether or not Eden was created along with the rest of the earth, clearly it was special to God, and it remains special to him. The presence of the tree of life in the New Jerusalem establishes that elements of Eden will again be part of the human experience. The presence of the tree of life in the present Heaven suggests that Heaven, too, has physical properties and is capable of containing physical objects. So the notion of paradise, which was so physical and visible in Eden, is not restricted to a "spiritual" or "invisible" presence in Heaven.

I remember the first time I went snorkeling. I saw countless fish of every shape, size, and color. And just when I thought I'd seen the most beautiful one of all, along came another one even more striking. Etched in my memory is a certain sound—the sound of a gasp going through my rubber snorkel as my eyes were opened to that breathtaking underwater world.

I imagine that our first glimpse of Heaven will likewise cause us to gasp in amazement and delight. That first gasp will likely be followed by many more as we continually encounter new sights in that endlessly wonderful place. And that will be just the beginning, because we will not see our real eternal home—the New Earth—until after our resurrection.

Doesn't paradise sound good to you right now?

Father, you made Eden a true paradise, bursting with life and colors and vibrancy. When people call Tahiti or Hawaii or the Bahamas "paradise," they are recognizing the true beauty that you created, but it is beauty that has faded under the ravages of the Curse. What will it be like to see true and undiminished beauty? What will it be like to be in your presence and behold stunning works of art you've created? If human art and music have so moved us, how much more will we be moved by your direct creation of art and music? If a universe under the Curse has so wowed us, how much more will we be amazed at a universe untouched by sin and suffering and death and corruption and disease? We can hardly wait, Lord. Fill us each day with anticipation. Use the longing within our hearts to help empower us to live in a way that brings you pleasure—you who are the source of all pleasure and delight.

SEEING EARTH FROM HEAVEN

There will be more rejoicing in heaven over one sinner who repents than over ninety-nine righteous persons who do not need to repent.   — Luke 15:7

We want something else which can hardly be put into words—to be united with the beauty we see, to pass into it, to receive it into ourselves, to bathe in it, to become part of it.[26]
— C. S. Lewis

Since martyrs in Heaven know that God hasn't yet brought judgment on their persecutors (Revelation 6:9-11), it seems evident that the inhabitants of the present Heaven can see what's happening on Earth, at least to some extent. In Revelation 18:20, when Babylon is brought down, an angel points to events happening on Earth and says, "Rejoice over her, O heaven! Rejoice, saints and apostles and prophets! God has judged her for the way she treated you." That the angel specifically addresses people living in Heaven indicates that they are aware of what's happening on Earth.

Further, there is "the roar of a great multitude in heaven shouting:

'Hallelujah!'" and praising God for specific events of judgment that have just taken place on Earth (Revelation 19:1-5). Again, the saints in Heaven are clearly observing what is happening.

Because Heaven's saints will return with Christ to set up his Kingdom on Earth (Revelation 19:11-14), it's hard to imagine that they would be ignorant of the culmination of human history. The depiction of saints in Heaven as blissfully unaware of what is happening on Earth seems inconceivable. After all, God and his angels (and the saints themselves) are about to return for the ultimate battle in the history of the universe, after which Christ will be crowned King. People on Earth may be oblivious to Heaven, but people in Heaven are *not* oblivious to Earth.

When King Saul wrongly appealed to the witch of Endor to call the prophet Samuel back from the afterlife, the medium was terrified when God actually sent him. But Samuel remembered what Saul had done before Samuel died, and he was aware of what had happened since (1 Samuel 28:3-8, 16-19). Though God could have briefed Samuel on all this, it seems likely the prophet knew these things simply because those in Heaven are aware of what happens on Earth.

When Moses and Elijah were called from Heaven to the Transfiguration on Earth, they "appeared in glorious splendor, talking with Jesus. They spoke about his departure, which he was about to bring to fulfillment at Jerusalem" (Luke 9:31). Moses and Elijah appear to have been fully aware of the drama they'd stepped into, of what was currently transpiring on Earth, and of God's redemptive plan about to be accomplished.

Hebrews 12:1 tells us to "run with perseverance the race marked out for us," creating the mental picture of the Greek competitions, which were watched intently by throngs of engrossed fans sitting high up in the ancient stadiums. The "great cloud of witnesses" refers to the saints who've gone before us, whose accomplishments on the playing field of life are now part of our rich history. The imagery may also suggest that those saints, the spiritual "athletes" of old, are now watching us and cheering us on from the great stadium of Heaven that looks down on the field of Earth. (The witnesses are said to *surround* us, not merely to have preceded us.)

In Heaven, Christ watches closely what happens on Earth, especially in the lives of his people (Revelation 2–3). If the sovereign God's attention is on Earth, *why wouldn't the attention of his people in Heaven be focused here as well?* When a great war is taking place, are those in the home country uninformed and unaware of it? Do those who know the writer, producer, and cast of a great drama—and who have an interest in the outcome—refrain from watching it?

Angels saw Christ on Earth (1 Timothy 3:16). There are clear indications that the angels know what is happening on Earth (1 Corinthians 4:9; 1 Timothy 5:21). If angels, why not saints? Surely God's people in Heaven would be as interested in spiritual events happening on Earth as angels are. Wouldn't we expect the body and bride of Christ in Heaven to be intensely interested in its counterpart still living on Earth?

Christ said, "There is rejoicing in the presence of the angels of God over one sinner who repents" (Luke 15:10). Notice it does not speak of rejoicing *by* the angels but *in the presence* of angels. Who is doing this rejoicing in Heaven? Logically, it would include God, but also the saints in Heaven, who would deeply appreciate the wonder of human conversion—especially the conversion of those they knew and loved on Earth.

If people in Heaven rejoice over conversions on Earth, then obviously *they must be aware of what is happening on Earth*—and not just generally, but specifically, down to the details of individuals coming to faith in Christ.

Many assume that people in Heaven must not be aware of anything on Earth or else they wouldn't be happy. But people in Heaven are not frail beings whose joy can be preserved only by shielding them from what's really going on in the universe!

Happiness in Heaven is not based on ignorance, but on perspective. Those in the presence of Christ will share God's perspective. God is full of joy, despite his awareness of what's happening on Earth, and despite his displeasure with certain things on Earth. Surely God's happiness is the prevailing mood of Heaven. We need not assume that happiness in Heaven is based on ignorance of Earth.

Do you know anyone now in Heaven who may be interested in whether you are following Christ? As they rejoiced at your conversion, do you think they may be celebrating your growth and obedience?

Father, thank you for the evidence that people in Heaven are aware of events on Earth and are cheering us on, rejoicing in your ongoing work of spiritual transformation. Thank you, too, that they have your perspective, and therefore nothing can diminish their happiness in you. We're also grateful that they, too, are longing for the final deliverance of the earth from sin and suffering and the Curse. Thank you that Jesus did the work that assures our ultimate deliverance from the Hell we deserve to the Heaven we don't deserve. We praise you for purchasing our redemption, even at such a price!

DAY 12

HEAVEN'S INHABITANTS: REMEMBERING AND PRAYING?

But Abraham replied, "Son, remember that in your lifetime you received your good things, while Lazarus received bad things, but now he is comforted here and you are in agony." — LUKE 16:25

Your soul has a curious shape because it is a hollow made to fit a particular swelling in the infinite contours of the divine substance, or a key to unlock one of the doors in the house with many mansions.[27] — C. S. LEWIS

In Heaven, those who endured bad things on Earth are comforted (Luke 16:25). This comfort implies a memory of what happened. If there is no memory of the bad things, what would be the need for, or nature of, such comfort?

After we die, we will give an account of our lives, down to specific actions and words (Matthew 12:36; 2 Corinthians 5:10). Given our improved minds and clear thinking, our memory should be more—not less—accurate concerning our earthly lives. How could we possibly give an account for what we can't remember?

Because we'll be held accountable for more than we presently remember, presumably our memory will have to be far better.

The doctrine of eternal rewards sheds light on Heaven dwellers' memories of their lives on Earth. In 1 Corinthians 3:12-15, we can see that our rewards hinge on specific acts of faithfulness done here that survive God's judgment of believers and are brought into Heaven with us. Our righteous deeds will not be forgotten but will follow us to Heaven (Revelation 14:13). The positions of authority and the treasures we're granted in Heaven will perpetually remind us of our lives here, because God will grant those rewards for what we do on Earth (Matthew 6:19-21; 19:21; Luke 12:33; 19:17, 19; 1 Timothy 6:19; Revelation 2:26-28).

God keeps a record in Heaven of what people, both unbelievers and believers, do on Earth. That record will outlast our earthly lives (2 Corinthians 5:10). For those now in Heaven, the records of life on Earth still exist. Malachi 3:16 says there's a "scroll of remembrance" that even now is being written in Heaven concerning those living on Earth.

Clearly, Heaven is a place for remembering, not forgetting.

Memory is a basic element of personality. If we are truly *ourselves* in Heaven, there must be continuity of memory from Earth to Heaven. We will not be different people, but the same people marvelously relocated and transformed. Heaven will cleanse us, but it will not revise or extinguish our origins or history. Undoubtedly, we will remember God's works of grace in our lives that comforted, assured, sustained, and empowered us to live for him.

What about the question of whether those in Heaven pray for us on Earth?

If people in Heaven remember their lives on Earth and are

allowed to see at least some of what happens, then it would seem strange for them *not* to be interceding for us in prayer. We know that at least one man who has died and gone to Heaven is now praying for us, because Romans 8:34 tells us that Jesus is at God's right hand, interceding for his people. If Jesus prays in Heaven, why wouldn't other people in Heaven pray?

The martyrs in Heaven also pray to God (Revelation 6:10), asking him to take specific action on Earth. They are praying for God's justice, which has intercessory implications for Christians now suffering here. The sense of connection and loyalty to the body of Christ—and concern for the saints on Earth—would likely be enhanced, not diminished, by being in Heaven (Ephesians 3:15). In any case, Revelation 6 makes it clear that some who have died and are now in Heaven are praying concerning what's happening here and now.

If prayer is simply talking to God, presumably we will pray more in Heaven than we do now—not less. Given our righteous state in Heaven, our prayers would be more effective than ever (James 5:16). Revelation 5:8 speaks of the "prayers of the saints" in a context that may include saints in Heaven. Of course, there is only "one mediator between God and men, the man Christ Jesus" (1 Timothy 2:5). We are never told to pray *for* the saints (in Heaven), or *to* the saints, or *through* the saints, but only to God, through his Son. But though we should not pray to the saints, the saints may well be praying for us.

Questions about our loved ones remembering us or possibly praying for us are rooted in our desire to be assured that our relationship with them continues even though we can't see them. But of that we can be certain. Though we naturally grieve the death of loved ones, we know that if they are believers, we will one day be reunited. As the apostle Paul writes, "We want you to know what will happen to the believers who have died so you will not grieve like people who have no hope. For since we believe that Jesus died and was raised to life again, we also believe that when Jesus returns, God will bring back with him the believers who have died" (1 Thessalonians 4:13-14, NLT). Their parting is not the end of our relationship with them, only an interruption. We have not "lost" them, because we know where they are. They are experiencing the joy of Christ's presence in a place so wonderful that Christ called it paradise.

Have you "lost" loved ones to Heaven? Does it encourage you to know where they are and that one day you'll be with them again, in the presence of Jesus and, eventually, on the New Earth?

Father, cause the hearts of your people to rejoice that we will one day be with you and with our Savior, Jesus. We praise you also that we will be reunited with our friends and family who know you and have gone before us into your presence. Thank you that they remember us, as we remember them. Until we see them again, comfort us with the knowledge that even now we are not disconnected from them. We have not lost them, and they have not lost us, because we know where they are and they know where we are. We look forward to our homecoming and the Great Reunion!

GOD'S PLAN TO REDEEM THE EARTH

Behold, I will create new heavens and a new earth.
— Isaiah 65:17

It is quite striking that virtually all of the basic words describing salvation in the Bible imply a return to an originally good state or situation.... The point of redemption is to free the prisoner from bondage, to give back the freedom he or she once enjoyed.[28]
— Albert Wolters

The entire physical universe was created for God's glory. When we rebelled, the universe fell under the weight of our sin. Yet God did not give up on us.

The serpent's seduction of Adam and Eve did not catch God by surprise. He had in place a plan by which he would redeem mankind—and all creation—from sin, corruption, and death. Just as he promises to make men and women new, he promises to renew the earth itself.

"'As the new heavens and the new earth that I make will endure before me,' declares the LORD, 'so will your name and descendants endure'" (Isaiah 66:22).

"In keeping with his promise we are looking forward to a new heaven and a new earth, the home of righteousness" (2 Peter 3:13).

"I saw a new heaven and a new earth, for the first heaven and the first earth had passed away" (Revelation 21:1).

Many other passages allude to the new heavens and New Earth without using those terms. God's redemptive plan culminates not at the return of Christ, nor in the millennial kingdom, but on the New Earth. Only then will all wrongs be made right. Only then will there be no more death, crying, or pain (Revelation 21:1-4).

Consider this: If God's plan were merely to take mankind to the present, intermediate Heaven, or to a Heaven that was the dwelling place of spirit beings, there would be no need for new heavens and a New Earth. Why refashion the stars of the heavens and the continents of the earth? God could simply destroy his original creation and put it all behind him. But he doesn't do that. Upon creating the heavens and the earth, he called it "very good" (Genesis 1:31). Not once has he renounced his claim on what he made.

God isn't going to abandon his creation. He's going to restore it. Earth's destruction will not be permanent but temporary. Just as our destroyed bodies will be raised as new bodies, the destroyed Earth will be raised as a New Earth. We won't go to Heaven and leave Earth behind. Rather, God will bring Heaven and Earth together into the same dimension, with no wall of separation, no armed angels to guard Heaven's perfection from sinful mankind (Genesis 3:24). God's perfect plan is "to bring all things in heaven and on earth together under one head, even Christ" (Ephesians 1:10).

God has never given up on his original creation. Yet somehow we've managed to overlook an entire biblical vocabulary that makes this point clear.

Reconcile. Redeem. Restore. Recover. Return. Renew. Regenerate. Resurrect. Each of these biblical words begins with the *re-* prefix, suggesting a return to an original condition that was ruined or lost. For example, *redemption* means to buy back what was formerly owned. Similarly, *reconciliation* means the restoration or re-establishment of a prior friendship or unity. *Renewal* means to make new again, restoring to an original state. *Resurrection* means becoming physically alive again, after death.

These words emphasize that God always sees us in light of what he intended us to be, and he always seeks to *restore us* to that design. Likewise, he sees the earth in terms of what he intended it to be, and he seeks to restore it to its original design.

In his excellent book *Creation Regained*, Albert Wolters writes, "[God] hangs on to his fallen original creation and salvages it. He refuses to abandon the work of his hands—in fact he sacrifices his own Son to save his original project. Humankind, which has botched its original mandate and the whole creation along with it, is given another chance in Christ; we are reinstated as God's managers on earth. The original good creation is to be restored."[29]

If God had wanted to consign Adam and Eve to Hell and start

over, he could have. But he didn't. Instead, he chose to redeem what he started with—the heavens, the earth, and mankind—to bring them back to his original purpose. God is the ultimate salvage artist. He loves to restore things—and make them even better.

"Ruined sinners to reclaim." This phrase from the hymn "Hallelujah, What a Savior!" reflects God's purpose in our salvation.[30] *Reclaim* is another *re-* word. It recognizes that God had a prior claim on humanity that was temporarily lost but is fully restored and taken to a new level in Christ. "The earth is the LORD's, and everything in it, the world, and all who live in it" (Psalm 24:1). God has never surrendered his title deed to the earth. He owns it—and he will not relinquish it to his enemies. In fact, Scripture tells us that "the reason the Son of God appeared was to destroy the devil's work" (1 John 3:8).

Note that it says Christ came not to destroy the *world* (which is *his* world) but to destroy the devil's *works*, which are to twist and pervert and ruin the world God made. Redemption will forever destroy the work of the devil by removing his hold on creation and by reversing the consequences. Far from destroying the world, God's plan is to *keep it from being destroyed* by Satan. God's plan is to remove the destruction that has already been inflicted on it. His plan is to redeem the world. God placed mankind on Earth to fill it, rule it, and develop it to God's glory. But that plan has never been fulfilled. Should we therefore conclude that God's plan was ill-conceived, thwarted, or abandoned? No. These conclusions do not fit the character of an all-knowing, all-wise, sovereign God. Second Peter 3 does *not* teach that God will destroy the earth and then be done with it. Rather, it promises that God will renew Heaven *and* Earth.

God is not some hapless inventor whose creation failed. He has a masterful plan, and he will *not* surrender us *or* the earth to the trash heap.

That makes me want to thank him right now. How about you?

☨ *God, expand our view of your greatness so that we may gain an appreciation for the greatness of your redemptive work. Thank you that you did not abandon us to Hell, but that you loved us enough to shed your divine blood to rescue us and our planet. Thank you that we have a future, and that Earth—from which you formed us, and over which you made us to rule—also has a future. Help us to anticipate that future today. And may our anticipation affect the decisions we make. We ask these things in the great name of our Redeemer, Jesus, the Lord of the earth.*

DAY 14

THE NEW EARTH: A REAL EARTH?

I will come back and take you to be with me that you also may be where I am. — JOHN 14:3

Everything will be glorified, even nature itself. And that seems to me to be the biblical teaching about the eternal state: that what we call heaven is life in this perfect world as God intended humanity to live it. When he put Adam in Paradise at the beginning, Adam fell, and all fell with him, but men and women are meant to live in the body, and will live in a glorified body in a glorified world, and God will be with them.[31] — MARTYN LLOYD-JONES

Many people can't resist spiritualizing what the Bible teaches about Heaven. According to an evangelical theologian, "While heaven is both a place and a state, it is primarily a state."[32] But what does this mean? Another theologian writes, "Paul does not think of heaven as a place, but thinks of it in terms of the presence of God."[33] But when a person is "present," doesn't that suggest there's a place?

One book puts *place* in quotation marks whenever it uses the word to describe Heaven or Hell. It says paradise is "a spiritual condition more than a spatial location."[34] But Jesus didn't say that Heaven was "primarily a state" or a "spiritual condition." He spoke of a *house* with many *rooms* and said he would prepare a *place* for us (John 14:2). In Revelation 21–22, the New Earth and New Jerusalem are portrayed as actual places, with detailed descriptions of the most substantial, physical substances, including hard and heavy precious stones. These depictions could not be more tangible!

Jesus told the disciples, "I will come back and take you to be with me that you also may be where I am" (John 14:3). He uses ordinary, earthly, spatial terms to describe Heaven. The word *where* refers to a place, a location. Likewise, the phrase "come back and take you" indicates movement toward a physical destination.

If Heaven isn't a place, would Jesus have said it was? If we reduce Heaven to something less than or other than a place, we strip Christ's words of their meaning.

Sometimes Christians have overstated the notion that we are aliens in this world. For instance, the old gospel song, "This world is not my home, I'm just a-passing through," conveys a half-truth. Yes, we may pass from the earth to the present Heaven through death, but eventually we'll be back to live forever on the restored Earth. We are pilgrims in this life, not because our home will *never* be on Earth, but because our ultimate home isn't on the present Earth (which is under the Curse). But just as the earth was once our intended home (before sin entered), it will one day again be our home (after sin is removed and the Curse is reversed).

Because the earth was damaged by our sin (Genesis 3:17), we have never known a world without corruption, suffering, and death. Yet we yearn for such a life and such a world. When we see a roaring waterfall, beautiful flowers, a wild animal in its native habitat, or the joy in the eyes of our pets when they see us, we sense that this world is—or at least was *meant to be*—our home.

Will the Eden we long for return? Will it be occupied by familiar, tangible, physical features and fully embodied people? The Bible clearly answers *yes*.

If we want to know what the ultimate Heaven, our eternal home, will be like, *the best place to start is by looking around us*. The present Earth is as much a valid reference point for envisioning the New Earth as our present bodies are for envisioning our new bodies. But can we look at the earth around us and imagine what it would be like to be unhindered by disease and death? Can we envision natural beauty untainted by destruction? Of course. People of all beliefs have long imagined such a world and have portrayed it in their art and literature and music.

The idea of the New Earth as a physical place isn't an invention of a wishful human imagination. Rather, it reflects the plans of a transcendent God, who made physical human beings to live on a physical Earth, and an immanent God, who chose to become a man on that same Earth. He did this that he might redeem mankind *and* Earth. Why? To glorify himself and enjoy forever the company of men and women in the world that he made for us.

To have a biblical worldview, we must have a sense of our past, present, and future, and how they relate to each other. Without understanding God's original plan for mankind and the earth, we cannot understand his future plan.

In the first two chapters of the Bible, God plants a garden on Earth; in the last two chapters of the Bible, he brings down the

New Jerusalem, with a garden at its center, to the New Earth. In Eden, there's no sin, death, or Curse; on the New Earth, there's *no more* sin, death, or Curse. In Genesis, the Redeemer is promised; in Revelation, the Redeemer returns. Genesis tells the story of paradise lost; Revelation tells the story of paradise regained. In Genesis, humanity's stewardship is squandered; in Revelation, humanity's stewardship is triumphant, empowered by the human and divine King Jesus.

These parallels are too remarkable to be anything but deliberate. These mirror images demonstrate the perfect symmetry of God's plan. We live in the in-between time, hearing echoes of Eden and the approaching footfalls of the New Earth.

Paul Marshall concludes, "This world is our home: we are made to live here. It has been devastated by sin, but God plans to put it right. Hence, we look forward with joy to newly restored bodies and to living in a newly restored heaven and earth. We can love this world because it is God's, and it will be healed, becoming at last what God intended from the beginning."[35]

Does it ring true to you that your home is not Earth in its present condition but Earth as it one day shall be?

Father, help us to be careful not to misstate our relationship to the earth. This is the home you made for us, and you will redeem it and refashion it into the New Earth, where we'll live forever. Thank you, Lord, that the earth matters. Thank you that our bodies matter. Thank you that animals and trees and rivers matter and that matter itself matters. Open our eyes to the fact that you have created all things and intended them to manifest your glory. Thank you again that you have not given up on your creation any more than you have given up on us.

THE COMING "RENEWAL OF ALL THINGS"

> At the renewal of all things, when the Son of Man sits on his glorious throne, you who have followed me will also sit on twelve thrones, judging the twelve tribes of Israel.
> — MATTHEW 19:28

We shall in the future world see the material forms of the new heavens and the new earth in such a way that we shall most distinctly recognize God everywhere present and governing all things, material as well as spiritual.[36] — AUGUSTINE

Peter preached that Jesus Christ "must remain in heaven until the time comes for God to restore everything, as he promised long ago through his holy prophets" (Acts 3:21).

What will be restored? *Everything*. (That's as broad and inclusive as it can be!)

What will happen to everything? It will be *restored*, returned to its original condition. Mankind will be restored to what we once were, what God designed us to be—fully embodied and righteous beings. The universe—the rest of *everything*—will be restored to what it once was. Can you imagine?

Where will this restoration take place? The answer, Peter tells us, is found in the promises given "long ago through [God's] holy prophets." Read the prophets and the answer becomes clear: God will restore everything *on Earth*. The prophets never spoke of some far-off realm of disembodied spirits. They were always concerned about the land, the inheritance, the city of Jerusalem, and the earth they walked on. This was their world, not some ghostly netherworld they'd never seen. Messiah, they correctly believed, would come from Heaven to Earth. Why? Not to take us away from Earth to Heaven, but to restore Earth to what he intended so he can live with us here forever.

When Anna, the prophetess, saw the baby Jesus, she immediately approached Mary and Joseph and "gave thanks to God and spoke about the child to all who were looking forward to the redemption of Jerusalem" (Luke 2:38).

Notice Luke's exact wording. What were God's people looking forward to? *Redemption.* Their own redemption? Of course. But it was much more than that. It was the redemption of not only themselves but also their families, their community, and specifically *their city*, Jerusalem. The redemption of Jerusalem implies the redemption of the whole nation. As the entire world was promised blessing through Abraham, the redemption of Jerusalem and Israel speaks of the redemption of the earth itself. This is why Scripture speaks of both the New Jerusalem and the New Earth.

Who would bring that redemption? Jesus, the Messiah, who would be King not only of redeemed individuals but also of a redeemed Jerusalem and a redeemed Earth. This is the gospel of the Kingdom of God. Anything less is a narrow view of God's redemptive plan. (Sadly, countless evangelical Christians believe this thin concept of salvation, limited to God's saving of individual human souls, without bodies and without the earth and the rest of God's creation.)

We need to allow Scripture to correct our mistaken theology. Will the earth as it is come to an end? Yes. To a *final* end? No.

Revelation 21:1 says the old Earth will pass away. But when people pass away, they do not cease to exist. So, just as *we* will be raised to be new people, *Earth* will be raised to be a New Earth.

When Peter spoke of all things being restored, he referred to the testimony of the prophets, but he had also heard it *directly from Christ*. When Peter pointed out to Jesus that the disciples had left everything to follow him, Jesus replied, "At the renewal of all things, when the Son of Man sits on his glorious throne, you who have followed me will also sit on twelve thrones, judging the twelve tribes of Israel" (Matthew 19:28).

Notice that Jesus did not say "after the *destruction* of all things," or "after the *abandonment* of all things," but "at the *renewal* of all things." This is not a small semantic point—it draws a line in the sand between two fundamentally different worldviews. Jesus explicitly said that "all things" would be "renewed."

The word *paligenesia*, translated "renewal" in Matthew 19:28, comes from two words that together mean "new genesis" or "coming back from death to life." When Jesus said that all things would be renewed, the disciples would have understood him to mean all things *on Earth*, the only place they knew.

If, because of the Fall, God would have given up on his original purpose for mankind to fill the earth and rule it (Genesis 1:28), he surely would not have repeated the same command to Noah after the Flood: "Be fruitful and increase in number and fill the earth" (Genesis 9:1). As long as the earth is still under sin and the Curse, people will be incapable of exercising proper stewardship of the earth. Yet that is still God's intention. He has not changed his plans.

God's stated purpose for us is to rule the earth forever as his children and heirs. Christ's mission was—and is—to redeem what was lost in the Fall and to destroy all competitors to God's dominion, authority, and power. When everything is put under his feet and mankind rules the earth as kings under Christ, the King of kings, everything will at last be as God intends. The era of rebellion will be over forever, and the redeemed universe, and all who serve Christ, will participate in the Master's joy!

As you face today's challenges, how does that make you feel?

Father, we look forward to the day when your will shall be done on Earth as it is in Heaven. We have never seen the world as you originally made it. But as you remake it, we will see and understand what a world full of righteousness and justice and love and grace really looks like. And it will be our home. Help us not to cling to the earth as it is today, under the Curse. Help us to long for the earth as you intended it and as it one day will be. Meanwhile, empower us to live as Christ's ambassadors, as citizens of a heavenly country. May people around us, seeing how citizens of this country live, be drawn to a better way, one that pleases you and satisfies them.

A VISION OF THE NEW EARTH

Your gates will always stand open, they will never be shut, day or night, so that men may bring you the wealth of the nations—their kings led in triumphal procession. ... I will make you the everlasting pride and the joy of all generations. — Isaiah 60:11, 15

Over and over again the Scriptures make this plain: the political power which has been so corrupted and twisted in the hands and hearts of sinful rulers must be returned to its rightful source.[37] — Richard Mouw

Isaiah 60 is a wonderful portrait of life on the New Earth. Though some of it appears to refer to the millennial kingdom—containing some things inconsistent with life on the New Earth—much of it foresees an eternal earthly kingdom, which could refer only to the New Earth.

Although Isaiah 60 doesn't contain the term *New Earth* (unlike Isaiah 65 and 66), we can be certain that Isaiah had the New Earth in mind, because John uses the exact language of Isaiah 60 in his depiction of the New Earth in Revelation 21–22. Thus, Isaiah 60 serves as a biblical commentary on John's portrayal of the New Earth. It is not, as a whole, restricted to the millennial kingdom.

At the beginning of Isaiah's remarkable, prophetic message, God says to his people in Jerusalem, "The LORD rises upon you and his glory appears over you. Nations will come to your light, and kings to the brightness of your dawn" (vv. 2-3). God's people will have a glorious future in which the earth's nations and kings will participate in and benefit from a renewed and glorious Jerusalem. It won't be only some nations, but all of them: "All assemble and come to you" (v. 4).

This will be a time of unprecedented rejoicing: "Then you will look and be radiant, your heart will throb and swell with joy" (v. 5). On the renewed Earth, the nations will bring their greatest treasures into this glorified city: "The wealth on the seas will be brought to you, to you the riches of the nations will come" (v. 5).

There will be animals on the New Earth, from various nations: "Herds of camels will cover your land, young camels of Midian and Ephah" (v. 6). Redeemed people will travel from far places to the glorified Jerusalem: "And all from Sheba will come, bearing gold and incense and proclaiming the praise of the LORD" (v. 6).

People who dwell on islands will worship God, and ships will come from "Tarshish, bringing your sons from afar, with their silver and gold, to the honor of the LORD your God, the Holy One of Israel, for he has endowed you with splendor" (v. 9).

Most of us are unaccustomed to thinking of nations, rulers, civilizations, and cultures in Heaven, but Isaiah 60 is one of many passages that demonstrate that the New Earth will in fact be *earthly*.

In verse 11, Isaiah speaks words that John (in Revelation 21:25-26) later applies directly to the New Jerusalem: "Your gates will always stand open, they will never be shut, day or night, so that men may bring you the wealth of the nations—their kings led in triumphal procession."

The magnificence of nations will be welcomed into the King's great city: "The glory of Lebanon will come to you, the pine, the fir and the cypress together" (v. 13). The hearts of the nations will be transformed in their attitudes toward God, his people, and his city: "The sons of your oppressors will come bowing before you; all who despise you will bow down at your feet and will call you the City of the LORD" (v. 14).

God assures the New Jerusalem, "I will make you the everlasting pride and the joy of all generations" (v. 15). This is not a temporary period of fleeting prosperity, but an *everlasting* condition. It will not be limited to one time period but will be for "all generations."

God promises something that has never yet been true of the earthly Jerusalem: "I will make peace your governor and righteousness your ruler. No longer will violence be heard in your land, nor ruin or destruction within your borders, but you will call your walls Salvation and your gates Praise" (vv. 17-18).

Isaiah then tells us, "The sun will no more be your light by day, nor will the brightness of the moon shine on you, for the LORD will be your everlasting light, and your God will be your glory. Your sun will never set again, and your moon will wane no more; the LORD will be your everlasting light, and your days of sorrow will end" (vv. 19-20). In Revelation 21:23 and 22:5, John uses much of the same wording, connecting Isaiah's prophecy directly to the New Earth.

Of the New Jerusalem, we're told that "nothing impure will ever enter it, nor will anyone who does what is shameful or deceitful, but only those whose names are written in the Lamb's book of life" (Revelation 21:27). Isaiah tells us the same thing, using inclusive language that could not apply to Earth under the Curse: "Then will all your people be righteous and they will possess the land [Earth] forever" (Isaiah 60:21). The earth will be theirs, not for a glorious decade or century or millennium, but *forever*.[38]

There is no reason to believe that the descriptions of the New Earth in Isaiah will be fulfilled any less literally than the prophecies about the Messiah in Isaiah 52–53. Because Isaiah's words about the Messiah's first coming were so meticulously fulfilled, down to specific physical details, shouldn't we assume that his subsequent prophecies concerning life on the New Earth will likewise be literally fulfilled?

Christ's millennial reign on the old Earth may anticipate the fulfillment of God's promises about Jerusalem's future. But we will see the ultimate fulfillment of these promises only in the New Jerusalem on the New Earth, when the Curse is gone, death is no more, and God's people are living on the earth forever.

"God is our refuge and strength, an ever-present help in trouble. Therefore we will not fear, though the earth give way and the mountains fall into the heart of the sea, though its waters roar and foam" (Psalm 46:1-3).

Even if you feel cast about in turbulent waters, can you see in your mind's eye the shores of a New Earth, one that will *never* give way?

⇌ *Father, your promises for our lives in this world are overwhelmingly wonderful. Help us not to spiritualize them and think they pertain only to another world, distant and fundamentally unlike our own. We long to live on Earth as you intended it to be, in bodies forever delivered from suffering, in a culture full of righteousness. We long to live according to your plan, doing work that is fulfilling, rewarding, and delightful. We long for the joy of learning, discovery, and adventures full of surprises. Thank you for the promise of the New Earth. Thank you that you are our primary joy and that drawing closer to you will be the highlight of every adventure. But we don't want to wait until we die to know you better and see you more clearly. Help us to do that right now, today.*

DAY 17

GOD'S GLORY ON GOD'S EARTH

They will neither harm nor destroy on all my holy mountain, for the earth will be full of the knowledge of the Lord as the waters cover the sea. In that day the Root of Jesse will stand as a banner for the peoples; the nations will rally to him, and his place of rest will be glorious.
— Isaiah 11:9-10

Heaven, as the eternal home of the divine Man and of all the redeemed members of the human race, must necessarily be thoroughly human in its structure, conditions, and activities.[39]
— A. A. Hodge

In reference to Earth under the Curse, God says, "The glory of the Lord fills the whole earth" (Numbers 14:21). But the universe will behold an even greater display of God's glory, one that will involve redeemed men and women and redeemed nations on a redeemed Earth. It is on Earth, God promises, that "the glory of the Lord will be revealed, and all mankind together will see it" (Isaiah 40:5). That God will be glorified on Earth is central to innumerable biblical prophecies, including the following:

"Surely his salvation is near those who fear him, that his glory may dwell in our land" (Psalm 85:9).

"I saw the glory of the God of Israel coming from the east . . . and the land was radiant with his glory" (Ezekiel 43:2).

In both passages, the word translated "land" (*erets*) is the word for "earth." Ezekiel saw God's glory at the gates of Jerusalem—manifested not in some immaterial realm but on the earth.

Many passages also promise that God's glory will be manifested to all the nations of the earth, particularly in the New Jerusalem:

"The nations will fear the name of the LORD, all the kings of the earth will revere your glory. For the LORD will rebuild Zion and appear in his glory" (Psalm 102:15-16).

"'They will proclaim my glory among the nations. And they will bring all your brothers, from all the nations, to my holy mountain in Jerusalem as an offering to the LORD—on horses, in chariots and wagons, and on mules and camels,' says the LORD" (Isaiah 66:19-20).

God's Kingdom and dominion are not about what happens in some remote, unearthly place; instead, they are about what happens on the earth, which God created for his glory. God has tied his glory to the earth and everything connected with it: mankind, animals, trees, rivers—*everything*.

Both Isaiah and John, using similar language, declare that on the New Earth "the kings of the earth will bring their splendor into" the New Jerusalem and "the glory and honor of the nations will be brought into it" (Revelation 21:24, 26; cf. Isaiah 60:3, 5).

In his excellent treatment of Isaiah and the New Jerusalem, *When the Kings Come Marching In*, Richard Mouw points out that the same ships of Tarshish and trees of Lebanon mentioned in Isaiah 60 are regarded elsewhere as objects of human pride that God promises to bring down (Isaiah 2:12-13, 16-18).

Isaiah speaks of a day of judgment in which "men will flee to caves in the rocks and to holes in the ground from dread of the LORD and the splendor of his majesty, when he rises to shake the earth" (2:19). This language is strongly evocative of the depiction of God's end times judgment, in which men try to hide "in caves and among the rocks of the mountains" (Revelation 6:15).

In Isaiah 10:34, the prophet tells us that God "will cut down the forest thickets with an ax; Lebanon will fall before the Mighty One." Because people put their pride and hope in "their" forests and ships, God will demonstrate his superiority by bringing down the forests and sinking the ships.

Now, if the trees of Lebanon and ships of Tarshish are singled out as being destroyed in God's future judgment, how can they, as Isaiah 60 indicates, turn up again in the Holy City as instruments of service to the Lord?

This is an example of a scriptural paradox in which the Bible simultaneously teaches about both destruction and renewal. Items that are now used for prideful and even idolatrous purposes will be used to the glory of God when the hearts of mankind are transformed and creation itself is renewed. There is nothing inherently wrong with ships, lumber, gold, or camels. What God will destroy in his judgment is the idolatrous *misuse* of these good things.

Then, having destroyed our perversions of his good gifts, he will, in his re-creation of the earth, restore these things as good and useful tools for his glory.

Theologian A. A. Hodge said it beautifully:

> Heaven, as the eternal home of the divine Man and of all the redeemed members of the human race, must necessarily be thoroughly human in its structure, conditions, and activities. Its joys and activities must all be rational, moral, emotional, voluntary and active. There must be the exercise of all the faculties, the gratification of all tastes, the development of all talent capacities, the realization of all ideals. . . . Heaven will prove the consummate flower and fruit of the whole creation and of all the history of the universe.[40]

Isn't that kind of Heaven a place you'd want to live in forever?

Father, thank you for the prophets who spoke through the crises and clouds of their day, seeing, with moments of clarity, the world you intend to shape from the ruins of this one. Their vision of a holy city, a holy country, a holy culture, and a holy Earth reverberate with hope and anticipation. Thank you that you will achieve Heaven on Earth, though we ourselves cannot. Earthly things that you created and that we turned into idols will be returned to their intended use: to glorify you forever. What a joy it will be to participate with you in a Kingdom that will never die, never be corrupted, and never disappoint.

DAY 18

THE CURSE REVERSED

No longer will there be any curse. — Revelation 22:3

No more let sins and sorrows grow
Nor thorns infest the ground;
He comes to make His blessings flow
Far as the Curse is found.
— Isaac Watts, "Joy to the World"

Just as God and mankind are reconciled in Christ, so too the dwellings of God and mankind—Heaven and Earth—will be reconciled in Christ, forever united in a new, physical universe where we will live as resurrected beings. The hymn "This Is My Father's World" expresses this truth in its final words: "Jesus who died shall be satisfied, and earth and heaven be one."[41]

Jesus Christ, as the God-man, forever links God's home—Heaven—with ours—Earth. As Ephesians 1:10 demonstrates, the idea of Earth and Heaven becoming one is explicitly biblical. Christ will make Earth into Heaven and Heaven into Earth.

Just as the wall that separates God and mankind is torn down in Jesus, so too the wall that separates Heaven and Earth will be forever demolished. There will be one universe, with all things in Heaven and on Earth together under one head, Jesus Christ. "Now the dwelling of God is with men, and he will live with them" (Revelation 21:3). God will live with us on the New Earth. That will "bring all things in heaven and on earth together." When God walked with Adam and Eve in the Garden, Earth was Heaven's backyard. The New Earth will be even more than that—it will be Heaven itself. And those who know Jesus will have the privilege of living there.

If the Bible said nothing else about life in the eternal Heaven (the New Earth), the words "no longer will there be any curse" would tell us a vast amount. After Adam sinned, God said, "Cursed is the ground [Earth] because of you" (Genesis 3:17). What would our lives be like if the Curse were lifted? One day we will know firsthand—but even now there's much to anticipate.

When the Curse is reversed, we will no longer engage in "painful toil" (v. 17). No longer will the earth yield "thorns and thistles" (v. 18), defying our dominion and repaying us for corrupting it. No longer will we "return to the ground . . . [from which we] were taken" (v. 19). No longer will we be swallowed up in death as unrighteous stewards who ruined ourselves and the earth.

As a result of the Curse, the first Adam could no longer eat from the tree of life, which presumably would have made him live forever in his sinful state (Genesis 3:22). Death, though a curse in itself, was also the only way out from under the Curse—and only because God had prepared a way to defeat death and restore mankind's relationship with him.

Christ came to remove the curse of sin and death (Romans 8:2). He is the last Adam, who will undo the damage wrought by the first (1 Corinthians 15:22, 45; Romans 5:15-19). In the Cross and the Resurrection, God made a way not only to restore his original design for mankind but also to expand it. In resurrected bodies, mankind will again dwell on Earth—a New Earth—completely free of the Curse. Unencumbered by sin, human activity will again lead naturally to a prosperous and magnificent culture.

Under the Curse, human culture has not been eliminated, but it has been twisted and severely hampered by sin, death, and decay. Before the Fall, food was readily available with minimal labor. Time was available to pursue thoughtful, aesthetic ideas, to work for the sheer pleasure of it, to please and glorify God by developing skills and abilities. Since the Fall, generations have lived and died after spending most of their productive years eking out an existence in the pursuit of food, shelter, and protection against theft and war. Mankind has been distracted and debilitated by sickness and sin. Our cultural development has likewise been stunted and warped, and sometimes misdirected.

Earth cannot be delivered from the Curse by being destroyed. It can be delivered only by being *resurrected*. The removal of the Curse will be as thorough and sweeping as the redemptive work of Christ. In bringing us salvation, Christ has already undone some of the damage in our hearts, but in the end he will finally and completely restore his entire creation to what God originally intended (Romans 8:19-21).

Christ's victory over the Curse will not be partial. Death will not just limp away to lick its wounds. It will be annihilated, utterly destroyed: "[God] will destroy the shroud that enfolds all peoples, the sheet that covers all nations; he will swallow up death forever. The sovereign LORD will wipe away the tears from all faces; he will remove the disgrace of his people from all the earth" (Isaiah 25:7-8).

Isaac Watts's magnificent hymn "Joy to the World" is theologically on target when it says that Christ comes to make his blessings flow "far as the curse is found." God will lift the Curse, not only morally (in terms of sin) and psychologically (in terms of sorrows), but also physically (in terms of thorns in the ground).

If redemption failed to reach the farthest boundaries of the Curse, it would be incomplete. The God who rules the world with truth and grace won't be satisfied until every sin, every sorrow, and every thorn is reckoned with. Christ's redemption extends to all that is under the Curse—Earth, plants, animals, everything.

We have never seen the earth as God made it. Our planet as we know it is a shadowy distortion of the original. But it does whet our appetites for the New Earth, doesn't it? If the present Earth—so damaged and diminished by the Curse—is at times so beautiful and wonderful and if our bodies—so damaged and diminished by the Curse—are at times overcome with a sense of the earth's beauty and wonder, then *how magnificent will the New Earth be?*

Are you looking forward to your resurrection? To the *earth's* resurrection?

☩ Father, we have never known life on Earth without the Curse. It has come to seem normal and permanent to us. Remind us that it is anything but normal. It is a

temporary aberration, a momentary rebellion that will decisively end. Our fallenness, and the earth's, is something that you have promised you will fix forever. Thank you for the promise that this earth we live on will one day be all you intended it to be. Help us look forward to that time and place when "no longer will there be any curse."[42]

DAY 19

OUR OLD BODIES MADE NEW

If Christ has not been raised, your faith is futile; you are still in your sins. Then those also who have fallen asleep in Christ are lost. If only for this life we have hope in Christ, we are to be pitied more than all men.
— 1 Corinthians 15:17-19

We will not be disembodied spirits in the world to come, but redeemed spirits, in redeemed bodies, in a redeemed universe.[43]
— R. A. Torrey

Paul says that if Christ hadn't risen from the dead, we'd still be in our sins—meaning we'd be bound for Hell, not Heaven.

He doesn't just say that if there's no *Heaven*, the Christian life is futile. He says that if there's no *resurrection of the dead*, then Christianity's hope is an illusion and we're to be pitied for placing our faith in Christ. Paul has no interest in a Heaven that's merely for human spirits.

Wishful thinking is not the reason why, deep in our hearts, we desire a resurrected life on a resurrected Earth instead of a disembodied existence in a spiritual realm. Rather, we desire it precisely because God intends for us to be raised to new life on the New Earth. It is God who created us to desire what we are made for. It is God who "set eternity in the hearts of men" (Ecclesiastes 3:11). It is God who designed us to live on Earth and to desire the earthly life. And it is our bodily resurrection that will allow us to return to an earthly life—this time freed from sin and the Curse.

"Therefore, if anyone is in Christ, he is a new creation; the old has gone, the new has come!" (2 Corinthians 5:17). Becoming a new creation sounds as if it involves a radical change, and indeed it does. But though we become *new* people when we come to Christ, we still remain the *same* people.

Conversion is a blend of change and continuity. When I became a Christian as a high school student, I became a new person, yet I was still the same person I'd always been. My mother saw a lot of changes, but she still recognized me. She said, "Good morning, Randy," not "Who are *you*?" I was still Randy Alcorn, though a substantially transformed Randy Alcorn. My dog never growled at me—he knew who I was.

Likewise, this same Randy (who is now very different) will undergo another change at death. And I will undergo yet *another* change at the resurrection. But through all the changes *I will still be who I was and who I am*. There will be continuity from this life to the next. I will be able to say with Job, "In my flesh I will see God; I myself will see him with my own eyes—I, and not another" (Job 19:26-27).

Conversion involves transforming the old, not eliminating it. Despite the radical changes that occur through salvation, death, and resurrection, we remain the unique beings that God created. We have the same history, appearance, memory, interests, and skills. This is the principle of *redemptive continuity*. God is not going to scrap his original creation and start over. Instead, he will take his fallen, corrupted children and restore, refresh, and renew us to our original design.

If we don't grasp the principle of redemptive continuity, we cannot understand the nature of resurrection. "There must be continuity," writes Anthony Hoekema, "for otherwise there would be little point in speaking about a resurrection at all. The calling into existence of a completely new set of people totally different from the present inhabitants of the earth would not be a resurrection."[44]

First Corinthians 15:53 says, "The perishable must clothe itself with the imperishable, and the mortal with immortality." *This* (the perishable and mortal) puts on *that* (the imperishable and immortal). Likewise, it is *we*, the very same people who walk this Earth, who will walk the New Earth. "*We* will be with the Lord forever" (1 Thessalonians 4:17, emphasis added).

The empty tomb is the ultimate proof that Christ's resurrection body was the same body that died on the cross. If *resurrection* meant the creation of a previously nonexistent body, Christ's original body would have remained in the tomb. When Jesus said to his disciples after his resurrection, "It is I myself," he was emphasizing to them that he was the same person—in spirit *and* body—who had gone to the cross (Luke 24:39). His disciples saw the marks of his crucifixion, unmistakable evidence that this was the same body.

Jesus said, "Destroy this temple, and I will raise it again in three days" (John 2:19). John clarifies that "the temple he had spoken of was his body" (v. 21). The body that rose is the body that was destroyed.

In its historic crystallization of orthodox doctrine, the Westminster *Larger Catechism* (1647) states, "The self-same bodies of the dead which were laid in the grave, being then again united to their souls forever, shall be raised up by the power of Christ."[45] The Westminster Confession, one of the great creeds of the Christian faith, says, "All the dead shall be raised up, with the self-same bodies, and none other."[46] "Self-same bodies" affirms the doctrine of continuity through resurrection.

This, then, is the most basic truth about our resurrected bodies: They are the same bodies God created for us, but they will be raised to greater perfection than we've ever known. We don't know everything about them, of course, but we do know a great deal. Scripture does not leave us in the dark about our resurrected bodies.

Because we each have a physical body, we already have the single best reference point for envisioning a *new* body. Likewise, the New Earth will still be Earth, but a changed Earth. It will be converted and resurrected, but it will still be Earth and recognizable as such. Just as those reborn through salvation maintain continuity with the people they were, so too the world will be reborn in continuity with the old world (Matthew 19:28).

When you picture the New Earth in your mind's eye, what do you see? Is it a vision that motivates you to serve God today, anticipating what he has planned for you?

⇛ *Father, we look forward to being who we are, yet very different, in Heaven. We look forward to our bodies functioning better and looking better and being better, but we're grateful they will still be our bodies. Thank you that you will fashion us into all that you have always planned that we should be.*

DAY 20

CHRIST'S RESURRECTION BODY: THE MODEL FOR OURS

The Lord Jesus Christ ... will transform our lowly bodies so that they will be like his glorious body.
— PHILIPPIANS 3:20-21

Somewhere in my broken, paralyzed body is the seed of what I shall become. The paralysis makes what I am to become all the more grand when you contrast atrophied, useless legs against splendorous resurrected legs. I'm convinced that if there are mirrors in heaven (and why not?), the image I'll see will be unmistakably "Joni," although a much better, brighter Joni.[47]
— JONI EARECKSON TADA

We can know a lot about our resurrection bodies. Why? Because we're told a great deal about Christ's resurrected body, and we're told that our bodies will be like his.

"Beloved, we are God's children now; it does not yet appear what we shall be, but we know that when he appears we shall be like him, for we shall see him as he is" (1 John 3:2, RSV).

"Just as we have borne the likeness of the earthly man, so shall we bear the likeness of the man from heaven" (1 Corinthians 15:49).

Though Jesus in his resurrected body proclaimed that he was not a ghost (Luke 24:39, NLT), countless Christians think they will be ghosts in the eternal Heaven. I know this because I've talked with many of them. They think they'll be disembodied spirits, or wraiths. The magnificent, cosmos-shaking victory of Christ's resurrection—by definition a physical triumph over physical death in a physical world—escapes them.

If Jesus had become a ghost, there would have been no resurrection, and redemption would not have been accomplished. But Jesus was not a ghost; he walked the earth in his resurrection body for forty days, showing us how we would live as resurrected human beings. In effect, he also demonstrated where we would live as resurrected human beings—on Earth. Christ's resurrection body was suited for life on Earth. As Jesus was raised to come back to live on Earth, we, too, will be raised to come back to live on Earth (1 Thessalonians 4:14; Revelation 21:1-3).

The risen Jesus walked and talked with two disciples on the Emmaus road (Luke 24:13-35). They asked him questions; he taught them and guided them in their understanding of Scripture. Though they didn't know it was Jesus until "their eyes were opened" (v. 31), suggesting that God prevented them from recognizing Christ, they saw nothing different enough in his appearance to suggest that his resurrected body looked any different from a normal human body. In other words, they perceived nothing amiss. They saw the resurrected Jesus as a normal, everyday human being. The soles of his feet didn't hover above the road—they walked on it.

We know that the resurrected Christ looked like a man because Mary called him "sir" when she assumed he was the gardener at the tomb (John 20:15). Jesus spent remarkably normal times with his disciples after his resurrection. Early one morning, he "stood on the shore" at a distance (John 21:4). He didn't hover or float—or even walk on water, though he could have. He called to the disciples (v. 5). He started a fire, and he was already cooking fish that he'd presumably caught himself. He cooked them, which means he didn't just snap his fingers and materialize a finished meal. He invited the disciples to add their fish to his and said, "Come and have breakfast" (John 21:12).

On another occasion, Christ suddenly appeared in a locked room where the disciples were gathered (John 20:19). His body could be touched and clung to and could consume food, yet it could apparently "materialize" as well. How is this possible? Could it be that a resurrection body is structured in such a way as to allow its molecules to pass through solid materials or to suddenly become visible or invisible?

We shouldn't assume that Christ's body will look *exactly* as it did before his death and resurrection, or that our bodies will look *exactly* as they do now. During Christ's transfiguration, the appearance of his face changed, and his clothing "became as bright as a flash of lightning" (Luke 9:29). Likewise, Elijah and Moses are described as appearing "in glorious splendor" (Luke 9:31).

Christ may literally shine in his Kingdom on the New Earth. John says of the city, "The Lamb is its lamp" (Revelation 21:23).

Christ appeared to Paul and blinded him on the road to Damascus (Acts 9:3-9).

Likewise, Scripture promises us that "the righteous will shine like the sun in the kingdom of their Father" (Matthew 13:43), and "will shine brightly like the brightness of the expanse of heaven . . . like the stars forever and ever" (Daniel 12:3, NASB).

Once we understand that Christ's resurrection is the prototype for the resurrection of mankind and the earth, we realize that Scripture has given us an interpretive key to understanding human resurrection and life on the New Earth. Shouldn't we interpret passages alluding to resurrected people living on the New Earth as literally as those concerning Christ's resurrected life during the forty days he walked on the old Earth?

When Paul speaks of our resurrection bodies, he says, "The body that is sown is perishable, it is raised imperishable; it is sown in dishonor, it is raised in glory; it is sown in weakness, it is raised in power; it is sown a natural body, it is raised a spiritual body. If there is a natural body, there is also a spiritual body" (1 Corinthians 15:42-44).

When Paul uses the term *spiritual body* (v. 44), he is not talking about a body made of spirit, or a nonphysical body—there is no such thing. A *body*, by definition, is physical—flesh and bones. The word *spiritual* here is an adjective that *describes* the body; it doesn't negate its meaning. A spiritual body is first and foremost a real body or it would not qualify to be called a body. If our bodies became spirits, Paul could have simply said, "It is sown a natural body, it is raised a spirit," but that's not what he says. Judging from Christ's resurrection body, a spiritual body looks and acts like a regular physical body most of the time, but it may have (and in

Christ's case it *does* have) some physical abilities beyond what is currently normal.

Many of us look forward to Heaven more now than we did when our bodies functioned well. Inside your body, even if it is broken or failing, is the blueprint for your resurrection body. You may not be satisfied with your current body or mind—but you'll be forever thrilled with your resurrection upgrade.

How does Christ's bodily resurrection affect your view of your future body and what life will be like on the New Earth?

☩ *Thank you, Father, for your promise of resurrected bodies and renewed minds, with which we will be better able to glorify and enjoy you forever. We aren't ready yet to appreciate the eternity of wonders you have prepared for us. But some days, Lord, we feel like we can't wait any longer. In your perfect timing, take us out of this fallen world, and bring us into your presence. And then, at the time you've appointed, send your Son back to this earth triumphant, to set up his Kingdom. And give us what we do not deserve: resurrected minds and bodies in perfect communion with you and our spiritual family. We long for the great banquet and the celebration that never ends. Come, Lord Jesus!*

DAY 21

AS MANKIND GOES, SO GOES CREATION

The creation waits in eager expectation for the sons of God to be revealed. For the creation was subjected to frustration . . . in hope that the creation itself will be liberated from its bondage to decay and brought into the glorious freedom of the children of God. We know that the whole creation has been groaning as in the pains of childbirth right up to the present time. Not only so, but we ourselves . . . groan inwardly as we wait eagerly for our adoption as sons, the redemption of our bodies.

— Romans 8:19-23

Even after the fall, the destiny and the redemption of the earth remain indissolubly united with the existence and development of the human race. The redemption of the earth is, in spite of all, still bound up with man. . . . Man is the instrument for the redemption of the earthly creation. And because this remains God's way and goal, there can be a new heaven and a new earth only after the great white throne, i.e. after the completion and conclusion of the history of human redemption.[48]

— Erich Sauer

Why does creation so eagerly await our resurrection? For one simple but critically important reason: *As mankind goes, so goes all of creation.* Just as all creation was spoiled through our rebellion, the deliverance of all creation hinges on our deliverance. The glorification of the universe hinges on the glorification of a redeemed human race. The destiny of all creation rides on our coattails.

What possible effect could our redemption have on galaxies that are billions of light-years away? The same effect that our fall had on them. Adam's and Eve's sins did not merely create a personal or localized catastrophe; it was a calamity of cosmic, not just global, proportions.

Astronomy was my childhood hobby. Years before I came to know Christ, I was fascinated by the violent collisions of galaxies, explosions of stars, and implosions into neutron stars and black holes. Entropy, the second law of thermodynamics, tells us that all things fall apart. Even the remotest parts of the universe reveal vast realms of fiery destruction.

But we should not look at things as they are now and assume they've always been this way. Isn't it reasonable to suppose that the pristine conditions of God's original creation were such that stellar energy would be replenished, planets would not fall out of orbit, and humans and animals would not die? What if God intended that our dominion over the earth would ultimately extend to the entire physical universe? Then we would not be surprised to see the entire creation come under the Curse, because it would all be under our stewardship.

Consider Paul's words about the central importance of Christ and the corresponding magnitude of his redemptive work: "God was pleased to have all his fullness dwell in [Christ], and through him to reconcile to himself *all things*, whether *things on earth* or *things in heaven*, by making peace through his blood, shed on the cross" (Colossians 1:19-20, emphasis added).

The gospel of God's Kingdom isn't good news just for us—it's good news for the animals, plants, stars, and planets. It's good news for the sky above and the earth below.

If we think of redemption too narrowly, we can be fooled into thinking that Heaven must be fundamentally different from Earth—because in our minds, Earth is bad, irredeemable, beyond hope. Indeed, "the teaching that the new creation involves a radically new beginning," writes theologian Cornelius Venema, "would suggest that sin and evil have become so much a part of the substance of the present created order that it is unrelievedly and radically evil. . . . It would even imply that the sinful rebellion of the creation had so ruined God's handiwork as to make it irretrievably wicked."[49] But let's not forget that God called the original Earth "very good"—the true Earth, as he designed it to be (Genesis 1:31).

The breadth and depth of Christ's redemptive work will escape us as long as we think it is limited to humanity. But as Paul explains,

> By him [Jesus] *all things* were created: *things in heaven and on earth*, visible and invisible, whether thrones or powers or rulers or authorities; *all things* were created by him and for him. He is before *all things*, and in him *all things* hold together. And he is the head of the body, the church; he is the beginning and the firstborn from among the dead,

so that in *everything* he might have the supremacy. For God was pleased to have all his fullness dwell in him, and through him to reconcile to himself *all things*, whether *things on earth* or *things in heaven*, by making peace through his blood, shed on the cross. (Colossians 1:16-20, emphasis added)

How will the effects of our bodily resurrection be felt by the entire universe? In exactly the same way that all creation suffered from our fall into sin. There is a direct connection, a metaphysical and moral link, between mankind and the physical universe.

Romans 8 contains a profound theological statement that extends the doctrine of the Fall far beyond what we might have expected. But in doing so, it extends the doctrine of Christ's redemption every bit as far.

We should expect that anything affected by the Fall will be restored to its original condition. Things will no longer get worse. When they change, they will only get better. That will be true of our bodies and our minds and human culture in the new universe. And there are no grounds to imagine that the God-created link between mankind and the physical universe will cease. Why shouldn't it continue for all eternity?

Many Christians seem to assume that the present universe will be permanently annihilated. But if this were the case, what analogy would we expect Paul to use for what will happen to creation? An old man dying? A mortally wounded soldier gasping his final breaths? Those images would fit well with a belief that the universe will come to a violent, final end. But Paul doesn't use analogies of death and destruction, he uses the analogy of childbirth: "The whole creation has been groaning as in the pains of childbirth right up to the present time" (Romans 8:22).

Does something in you long for the coming redemption? Look at other people; listen to the cries of animals, to the oceans, and to the wind in the trees. Do you see and hear evidence of this groaning for something better . . . for the world to be made right at last?

☫ *Thank you, Lord, that a far better world will be reborn out of this one, because sometimes we are so weary of this world the way it is. We praise you, Lord, for the extent of your redemptive work and how it points to the wonders of your character and your love. We are so excited to know there is an eternal future ahead for your creation, which we have yet to see as you intended it. Yet if its beauty can sometimes shine so brightly even under the dark clouds of the Curse, what will it be like to see it in all its glory? Thank you that you are far bigger and greater than we have imagined and that your redemptive work is likewise far bigger and greater.*

DAY 22

WHAT THE "NEW" IN "NEW EARTH" MEANS

I saw a new heaven and a new earth. . . . I saw the Holy City, the new Jerusalem, coming down out of heaven from God. — REVELATION 21:1-2

New creation is the dominating notion of biblical theology because new creation is the goal or purpose of God's redemptive-historical plan; new creation is the logical main point of Scripture.[50] — GREG BEALE

When Scripture speaks of a "new song," do we imagine something that is wordless, silent, or without rhythm? Of course not. Why? Because *it wouldn't be a song*.

If I promised you a new car, would you say, "If it's new, it probably won't have an engine, a transmission, doors, wheels, windows, or upholstery"? No, you'd never make such assumptions. Why? Because if a new car didn't have these things, *it wouldn't be a car*.

Likewise, when Scripture speaks of a new Earth, we can expect that it will be a far better version of the old Earth, but *it will truly be Earth*. By calling it the New *Earth*, God emphatically tells us it will be earthly and, thus, familiar. Otherwise, why call it Earth? Why not call it a new kingdom or empire or territory or dwelling place?

The word *new* is an adjective. Adjectives modify nouns, but they don't negate them. The noun is always the main thing. Thus, a new car is first and foremost a car; a new body is first a body; and a new Earth is first an Earth.

The Bible begins with this powerful statement: "In the beginning God created the heavens and the earth" (Genesis 1:1). "The heavens and the earth" is a biblical designation for the entire universe. So when Isaiah 65 and 66, 2 Peter 3, and Revelation 21 all speak of "new heaven(s) and a new earth," they indicate a transformation of the entire universe.

In Revelation 21:1, the Greek word *kainos*, translated "new" in the term *New Earth*, means new "in the sense that what is old has become obsolete, and should be replaced by what is new. In such a case the new is, as a rule, superior in kind to the old."[51]

Paul uses the same word, *kainos*, when he speaks of a believer in Christ becoming "a new creation" (2 Corinthians 5:17). The believer is still the same person as before, but he or she has been made new. Likewise, the New Earth will be the same as the old Earth, but made new.

In our resurrection, God may gather the scattered DNA and atoms and molecules of our dead and decayed bodies. In the earth's resurrection, he will regather all he needs of the scorched and disfigured Earth. As our old bodies will be raised to new bodies, so the old Earth will be raised to become the New Earth.

So, will the earth be *destroyed* or *renewed*? The answer is *both*—

but the destruction will be temporal and partial, whereas the renewal will be eternal and complete. Those who emphasize our citizenship in Heaven—and I'm one of them—sometimes have an unfortunate habit of minimizing our connection to the earth and our destiny to live on it and rule it. We end up thinking of eternity as a non-earthly spiritual state in which Earth is at best a distant memory.

Understanding and anticipating the physical nature of the New Earth corrects a multitude of errors. It frees us to love, without guilt, the world that God has made, while saying no to that world corrupted by our sin. It reminds us that God himself gave us the earth, gave us a *love* for the earth, and will give us the New Earth.

Think what this will mean for Adam and Eve. When the New Earth comes down from Heaven, the rest of us will be going home, but Adam and Eve will be *coming* home. Only they will have lived on three Earths—one unfallen, one fallen, and one redeemed. Only they will have experienced, at least to a degree, the treasure of an original, magnificent Earth that was lost and is now regained.

When we open our eyes for the first time on the New Earth, will it be unfamiliar, or will we recognize it as home?

As human beings, we long for home, even as we step out to explore new frontiers. We long for the familiarity of the old, even as we crave the innovation of the new. Think of all the things we enjoy that are new: moving into a new house, the smell of a new car, the feel of a new book, watching a new movie, hearing a new song, the pleasure of a new friend, the enjoyment of a new pet, receiving new presents on our birthday, staying in a new hotel room, arriving at a new school or a new workplace, welcoming a new child or grandchild, eating new foods that suit our tastes.

We love newness—yet in each case, what is new is attached to something familiar. We don't really like things that are utterly foreign to us. Instead, we appreciate fresh and innovative variations on things that we already know and love.

When we hear that in Heaven we will have new bodies and live on a New Earth, that's how we should understand the word *new*—a restored and perfected version of our familiar bodies and our familiar Earth.

If someone asked you what the term *New Earth* means, how would you answer?

Lord, it's overwhelming to think that just as you will make us new in the final Resurrection, you will also make the earth new. We love the earth. We wish it weren't so messed up; we would love to live on an Earth without sin and death and suffering. We would love to enjoy nature without natural disasters or animal attacks, poison ivy or forest fires, or injuries from falling. Thank you that you didn't make a mistake when you created the earth and created us. Thank you that you will make a new us and a New Earth that will bring you glory and joy—a joy that you desire for us to share with you forever.

DAY 23

HOMESICK FOR HEAVEN

> In keeping with his promise we are looking forward to a new heaven and a new earth, the home of righteousness.
> — 2 Peter 3:13

> *When I heard that I was in the wrong place ... my soul sang for joy, like a bird in spring. I knew now ... why I could feel homesick at home.*[52] — G. K. Chesterton

Do you recall a time when you were away from home and desperately missed it? Maybe it was when you were at college or in the military, were traveling extensively overseas, or needed to move because of a job. Do you remember how your heart ached for home? That's how we should feel about Heaven. We are a displaced people, longing for our home. C. S. Lewis said, "If I find in myself a desire which no experience in this world can satisfy, the most probable explanation is that I was made for another world."[53]

Nothing is more often misdiagnosed than our homesickness for Heaven. We think that what we want is sex, drugs, alcohol, a new job, a raise, a doctorate, a spouse, a large-screen television, a new car, a cabin in the woods, a condo in Hawaii. What we really want is the person we were made for, Jesus, and the place we were made for, Heaven. Nothing less can satisfy us.

I like G. K. Chesterton's picture of feeling homesick at home. We can say, "Heaven will be our eternal home," or "Earth will be our eternal home," but we shouldn't say, "Heaven, not Earth, will be our eternal home," because the Heaven in which we'll live permanently will be on the New Earth.

Years ago, a Christian I met in passing told me it troubled him that he really didn't long for Heaven. Instead, he yearned for an Earth that was like God meant it to be. He didn't desire a Heaven out there somewhere, but an Earth under his feet, where God was glorified and he could fellowship with and serve God forever. He felt profoundly guilty and unspiritual for this desire.

At the time, my eyes hadn't been opened to Scripture's promise of the New Earth. If I could talk with that man again (I hope he reads this), I'd tell him what I should have told him then—that his desire was biblical and right. In fact, the place he's always longed for, an Earth where God is fully glorified, is the very place where he will live forever.

Christ's incarnation brought Heaven down to Earth. The coming New Earth will be God's permanent dwelling place, as pure and holy as Heaven has ever been. Thus, it cannot be inappropriate to think of Heaven in earthly terms, because Scripture itself compels us to do so. Paul Marshall writes, "What we need is not to be rescued from the world, not to cease being human, not to stop caring for the world, not to stop shaping human culture. What we need is the power to do these things according to the will of God. We, as well as the rest of creation, need to be redeemed."[54]

To say "This world is not your home" to a person who's alive and alert to the wonders of the world is like throwing a bucket of water on a blazing fire. We should be fanning the flames of that fire to help it spread, not seeking to put it out. Otherwise, we malign our God-given instinct to love the earthly home that God himself made for us. And we reduce "spirituality" to a denial of art, culture, science, sports, education, and everything else human.

When we do this, we set ourselves up for hypocrisy—for we may pretend to disdain the world while sitting in church, but when we get in the car, we turn on our favorite music and head home to barbecue with friends, watch a ball game, play golf, ride bikes, work in the garden, or curl up with a cup of coffee and a good book. We do these things not because we are sinners but because we are *people*. We will still be people when we die and go to Heaven. This isn't a disappointing reality—it's God's plan. He made us as we are—except the sin part, which has nothing to do with friends, eating, sports, gardening, or reading.

Like you, I'm tired of sin and suffering and crime and death and most of the things on the evening news. I'm tired of living with myself as I now am. But I love towering waterfalls crashing on rocks below. I love the spaciousness of the night sky over the desert. I love playing tennis and riding my bike and snorkeling in clear waters, as the physical person God has made me. I love the coziness of sitting next to Nanci on the couch in front of the fireplace, blanket over us and dog snuggled next to us.

These experiences are not Heaven—but they are little glimpses and *foretastes* of Heaven. What we love about this life are the things that resonate with the life God made us for. The things we love are not merely the best this life has to offer—they are previews of the greater life to come.

Do you ever feel homesick for Heaven?

Thank you, Father, for this great Earth. Remind us that the earth wasn't made by Satan, to mock and oppose you. Rather, it was made by you to bring you glory. Thank you that you have made us physical beings, connected to the earth. Thank you that our destiny is to live on a renewed Earth, cleansed of sin and all that's wrong. Thank you that the wonders of creation, which declare your glory, will not disappear but will re-emerge on the New Earth as greater testimonies to your glory than we can now imagine.

DAY 24

THE JOY OF LIVING WITH GOD FOREVER

I will put my dwelling place among you.... I will walk among you and be your God, and you will be my people.
— Leviticus 26:11-12

If the goodness, beauty, and wonder of creatures are so delightful to the human mind, the fountainhead of God's own goodness (compared with the trickles of goodness found in creatures) will draw excited human minds entirely to itself.
— Thomas Aquinas

In Eden, God came down to Earth, the home of mankind, whenever he wished (Genesis 3:8). On the New Earth, God and mankind will be able to come to each other whenever they wish. We will not have to leave our home to visit God. He will not have to leave his home to visit us. God and mankind will live together forever in the same home—the New Earth.

God says, "My dwelling place will be with them; I will be their God, and they will be my people" (Ezekiel 37:27) and "I will live with them and walk among them, and I will be their God, and they will be my people" (2 Corinthians 6:16).

Consider this statement: "God himself will be with them" (Revelation 21:3). Why does it emphatically say God *himself*? Because God won't merely send us a delegate. He will actually come to live among us on the New Earth.

God's glory will be the air we breathe, which will make us want to breathe deeper. In the new universe, we'll never be able to travel far enough to leave God's presence. Wherever we go, God will be there. However great the wonders of Heaven, God himself is Heaven's greatest prize.

In Heaven, we'll at last be freed of self-righteousness and self-deceit. We'll no longer question God's goodness; we'll see it, savor it, enjoy it, and declare it to our companions. Surely we will wonder how we ever could have doubted his goodness. For then our faith will be sight—*we shall see God.*

Jonathan Edwards said in a 1733 sermon, "God is the highest good of the reasonable creature, and the enjoyment of him is the only happiness with which our souls can be satisfied. To go to heaven fully to enjoy God, is infinitely better than the most pleasant accommodations here."

Many books and programs these days talk about messages from the spirit realm, supposedly from people who've died and now speak through channelers or mediums. They claim to have come from Heaven to interact with loved ones, yet they almost never talk about God or express wonder at seeing Jesus. But no one who had actually been in Heaven would neglect to mention what Scripture shows to be Heaven's main focus: God himself. If you had spent an evening dining with a king, you wouldn't come back and talk about the wall hangings and place settings; you'd talk about the king. When Heaven was revealed to the apostle John, he recorded the details, but first and foremost, from beginning to end, he kept talking about Jesus.

The best-selling novel *The Five People You Meet in Heaven* portrays a man who dies, goes to Heaven, and meets five people who tell him his life really mattered. He discovers forgiveness and acceptance. It sounds good, but the book fails to present Jesus as the object of saving faith. It portrays a "Heaven" that isn't about God, but about us. God is not the main person we meet in this "Heaven"—he's not even one of five people we meet there! That is why the "Heaven" portrayed in the book is ultimately shallow and unsatisfying.

Going to Heaven without God would be like a bride going on her honeymoon without her groom. If there's no God, there's no Heaven. Teresa of Avila said, "Wherever God is, there is Heaven."[55] The corollary is obvious: Wherever God is not, is Hell. Heaven will simply be a physical extension of God's goodness. To be with God—to know him, to see him—is the central, irreducible draw of Heaven.

Jesus promised his disciples, "I will come back and take you to be with me that you also may be where I am" (John 14:3). For Christians, to die is "to be present with the Lord" (2 Corinthians 5:8, NKJV). The apostle Paul says, "I desire to depart and be with Christ, which is better by far" (Philippians 1:23). He could have said, "I desire to depart and be in Heaven," but he didn't. His mind was on being with his Lord Jesus, which is the most significant aspect of Heaven.

When Jesus prayed that we would be with him in Heaven,

he explained why: "Father, I want those you have given me to be with me where I am, and *to see my glory*, the glory you have given me because you loved me before the creation of the world" (John 17:24, emphasis added). When we accomplish something, we want to share it with those closest to us. Likewise, Jesus wants to share his glory with us—his person and his accomplishments.

Christ's desire for us to see his glory should touch us deeply. What an unexpected compliment that the Creator of the universe has gone to such great lengths, at such sacrifice, to prepare a place for us where we can behold and participate in his glory.

Have you ever imagined what it would be like to walk the earth with Jesus, as the disciples did? If you know Christ, you *will* have that opportunity—on the New Earth. Whatever we will do with Jesus, we'll be doing with the second member of the triune God. What will it be like to run beside God, laugh with God, discuss a book with God, sing and climb and swim and play catch with God? Jesus promised we would eat with him in his Kingdom. This is an intimacy with God unthinkable to any who don't grasp the significance of the Incarnation. Think of it—to eat a meal with Jesus will be to eat a meal *with God*.

The infinitely fascinating God is by far the most important and most interesting person we'll ever meet in Heaven.

The good news is that we can get to know this captivating God here and now. We do this when we come before him humbly in prayer, confess our failings, read and contemplate his Word, and gather together in Bible-teaching churches with other followers of Jesus.

Are you doing what it takes to get to know God? What else can you do?

⇒ *God, free us from human-centered views of Heaven. These lead to a superficial view of Heaven that is unworthy of you, the King and core of Heaven. Help us see that as the sun is the center of the solar system, you are the center of Heaven, the center of the universe. It's about you. We will be happily held in the gravitational pull of your infinite being, finding our joy not in self-affirming remedies, but in knowing, worshiping, serving, and enjoying you!*

PROMISED LAND, PROMISED EARTH: THE NEW EARTH VS. THE MILLENNIUM

> Evildoers shall be cut off; but those who wait on the LORD, they shall inherit the earth. . . . The meek shall inherit the earth, and shall delight themselves in the abundance of peace. — PSALM 37:9-11, NKJV

Why do we not know the country whose citizens we are? Because we have wandered so far away that we have forgotten it. But the Lord Christ, the king of the land, came down to us, and drove forgetfulness from our hearts. God took to Himself our flesh so that He might be our way back. — AUGUSTINE

If you were to describe a kingdom, what elements would you include? A king, certainly, and subjects to be ruled. Anything else?

To be rightly described as a kingdom, wouldn't it also have to include *territory? government? culture?*

Why is it, then, that when we think of God's Kingdom, we

often think only of the King and his subjects? Perhaps we assume that the only leader will be the King—but have you ever heard of such a thing? Don't kings *always* delegate their rule to subordinate leaders who serve under them? We might suppose that the sovereign God would be an exception to this and that he would rule his Kingdom all by himself, delegating nothing. But this supposition is wrong. Scripture repeatedly shows God to be a delegator, the *original* delegator. He explicitly and repeatedly declares his design that his people will rule the earth under him.

What about culture? Can you conceive of a kingdom that involves people in relation to their king and to one another but does *not* involve the social, relational, creative, and interactive context we know as culture?

Strangest of all, we often think of God's Kingdom without envisioning a *territory*. We tend to spiritualize God's Kingdom, perceiving it as otherworldly, intangible, and invisible. But Scripture tells us otherwise.

Revelation 5:1-10 depicts a powerful scene in the present Heaven. God the Father, the ruler of Heaven, sits on the throne with a sealed scroll in his right hand. What's sealed—with seven seals, to avoid any possibility that the document has been tampered with—is the Father's will, his plan for the distribution and management of his estate. In this case, the entitlement of the estate is the earth, which includes its inhabitants. God had intended for the world to be ruled by humans. But who will come forward to open the document and receive the inheritance? Jesus, the Messiah, the God-man, who will take the earth and rule it as his inheritance.

This future King was slain that he might purchase "men for

God"—and not just a small representation of fallen humanity, but "from every tribe and language and people and nation" (Revelation 5:9).

The passage culminates with a statement about Christ's followers: "You have made them to be a kingdom and priests to serve our God, and they will reign on the earth" (Revelation 5:10).

An essential component of any kingdom is *land*. The earth is the land we will rule, righteously exercising dominion over it as God first commanded Adam and Eve to do.

We are pilgrims on this earth, which is passing away, but eventually we'll be pioneers and settlers on the New Earth. The earth is our proper dwelling place: "For the upright will live in the land, and the blameless will remain in it; but the wicked will be cut off from the land" (Proverbs 2:21-22). "The righteous will never be uprooted, but the wicked will not remain in the land" (Proverbs 10:30).

Isaiah and the prophets make clear the destiny of God's people. They will live in righteousness and peace and prosperity, as free people in the land that God promised them.

But what about all the recipients of these promises who have died—including people who lived in times of enslavement and captivity, war, poverty, and sickness? For many of them, life was short, hard, and cruel. Did these poor people ever live to see peace and prosperity, a reign of righteousness, or the end of wickedness?

No.

Have any of their descendants lived to see such a place?

No.

> All these people were still living by faith when they died. They did not receive the things promised; they only saw them and welcomed them from a distance. And they admitted that they were aliens and strangers on earth. People who say such things show that they are looking for a country of their own. . . . They were longing for a better country—a heavenly one. . . . [God] has prepared a city for them (Hebrews 11:13-14, 16).

The "country of their own" spoken of in Hebrews 11 is a real country, with a real capital city, the New Jerusalem. It is an actual place where these "aliens and strangers on earth" will ultimately live in actual bodies. If the promises that God made to them were promises on Earth and regarding Earth (and certainly they were), then the heavenly "country of their own" must ultimately include Earth. The fulfillment of these prophecies requires exactly what Scripture elsewhere promises—a resurrection of God's people and God's Earth.

What thrilled these expectant believers was not that God would rule in *Heaven*—he already did. What fueled their hope in the hardest of times was that one day God would rule on *Earth*; that he would forever remove sin, death, suffering, poverty, and heartache. They believed the Messiah would come to Earth, and in doing so bring Heaven to Earth. The Messiah would make God's will be done on Earth as it is in Heaven.

Some believers have come to imagine that these promises are limited to what is called the millennial kingdom. But though those promises may *sometimes* speak of the Millennium, in fact they speak of much more: the New Earth.

Revelation 20 refers six times to the Millennium, describing it like this:

- The devil is bound for a thousand years (v. 2);
- For a thousand years, the nations are no longer deceived (v. 3);
- The martyrs come to life and reign with Christ for a thousand years (v. 4);
- The rest of the dead don't come to life until after the thousand years are ended (v. 5);
- The saints will be priests and kings for a thousand years (v. 6);
- Satan will be loosed at the end of the thousand years, and he will prompt a final human rebellion against God (vv. 7-8).

Theologians differ over whether the Millennium should be understood as a literal thousand-year reign, and when it will occur in relation to the second coming of Christ.

Some believe the Millennium is occurring now as Christ's people reign with him in the present Heaven. Others believe the Millennium will be a literal kingdom on the present Earth, a final era of peace and prosperity under Christ's rule. They believe there will still be some death and sin, though much less, and that there will be a final human rebellion against Christ. Then, after the final judgment is complete, God will at last renew the heavens and the earth, after which there will be no sin or suffering or death.

I attended schools that teach a literal Millennium, and I tend to embrace that viewpoint, though I have studied and understand the merits of other perspectives. But Christians can disagree about the Millennium while fully agreeing about the New Earth. The Millennium question relates to whether the old Earth will end soon after the return of Christ, or a thousand years later after the end of the Millennium. But regardless of when the old Earth ends, the central fact is this: *the New Earth will begin, and it will last forever.* The Bible is emphatic that God's ultimate kingdom and our final home will *not* be on the old Earth but on the New Earth, where at last God's original design will be fulfilled and enjoyed *forever*—not just for a thousand years.

Christ says that he will write his own name on those who overcome, as well as "the name of my God and the name of the city of my God, the new Jerusalem, which is coming down out of heaven from my God" (Revelation 3:12). Both God (the person) and the New Jerusalem, the city of God (the place), are spoken of as the primary ways of identifying (naming) the followers of Jesus. Our very identity is wrapped up in the place of our destiny: the New Jerusalem, on the New Earth.

After saying that mankind would rise from the dust of the earth (Daniel 12:2-3), God promises Daniel, "You will rise to receive your allotted inheritance" (Daniel 12:13). Inheritance involves land, a place lived on and managed by human beings. The New Earth is the ultimate Promised Land. It will be the eternal Holy Land in which all God's people will dwell.

Are you looking forward to an imperishable inheritance on the New Earth?

☧ *Lord, you are our greatest inheritance, but we thank you, too, for our coming inheritance of actual land, a vast estate called the New Earth. Thank you that we will forever enjoy it, one another, and you. Thank you that we will fulfill your desire by ruling over that great land. Help us to live today as your humble servants... as the meek who will one day inherit the earth.*

THE KINGDOM OF KINGDOMS

He was given authority, glory and sovereign power; all peoples, nations and men of every language worshiped him. His dominion is an everlasting dominion that will not pass away, and his kingdom is one that will never be destroyed. — DANIEL 7:14

In the messianic kingdom the martyrs will reclaim the world as the possession which was denied to them by their persecutors. In the creation in which they endured servitude, they will eventually reign.[56] — IRENAEUS

God created Adam and Eve to be king and queen over the earth. Their job was to rule the earth to the glory of God. They failed.

Jesus Christ is the second and last Adam, and the church is his bride, the second Eve. Christ is King, the church is his queen. He will exercise dominion over all nations of the earth: "He will rule from sea to sea and from the River to the ends of the earth. . . . All kings will bow down to him and all nations will serve him" (Psalm 72:8, 11). As the new head of the human race, Christ will at last accomplish what was entrusted to Adam and Eve—with his beloved people as his bride and co-rulers. God's saints will fulfill on the New Earth the role that God first assigned to Adam and Eve on the old Earth. "They will reign for ever and ever" (Revelation 22:5).

Human kingdoms will rise and fall until Christ brings to Earth a Kingdom where mankind will rule in righteousness. Daniel prophesied, "In the time of those kings, the God of heaven will set up a kingdom that will never be destroyed, nor will it be left to another people. It will crush all those kingdoms and bring them to an end, but it will itself endure forever" (Daniel 2:44).

As Christ will be the King of kings, his realm will be the Kingdom of kingdoms—the greatest kingdom in human history. Yes, *human history*, for our history will not end at Christ's return or upon our relocation to the New Earth; it will continue forever, to the glory of God.

"Rejoice greatly. . . . See, your king comes to you, righteous and having salvation, gentle and riding on a donkey, on a colt, the foal of a donkey. . . . He will proclaim peace to the nations. His rule will extend from sea to sea and from the River to the ends of the earth" (Zechariah 9:9-10). Matthew 21:5 makes it clear that Zechariah's prophecy concerns the Messiah. Just as the first part of the prophecy was literally fulfilled when Jesus rode a donkey into Jerusalem, we should expect that the second part will be literally fulfilled when Jesus brings peace to the nations and rules them all. Jesus will return to Earth as "King of kings and Lord of lords" (Revelation 19:11-16). We're promised that "the LORD will be king over the whole earth" (Zechariah 14:9).

Bible-believing Jews in the first century were not foolish to think that the Messiah would be King of the earth. They were wrong about the Messiah's identity when they rejected Christ, and they were wrong to overlook his need to come as a suffering servant to redeem the world; but they were *right* to believe that the Messiah would forever rule the earth. He will!

In his parables, Jesus speaks of our ruling over cities (Luke 19:17). Paul addresses the subject of Christians ruling as if it were Theology 101: "Do you not know that the saints will judge [or rule] the world? . . . Do you not know that we will judge [or rule] angels?" (1 Corinthians 6:2-3). The form of the verb in these questions implies that we won't simply judge them a single time but will continually rule them.

If Paul speaks of this future reality as if it were something every child should know, why is it so foreign to Christians today? Elsewhere he says, "If we endure, we will also reign with him" (2 Timothy 2:12). God's decree that "[his servants] will reign for ever and ever" on the New Earth (Revelation 22:5) is a direct fulfillment of the commission he gave to Adam and Eve: "Be fruitful and increase in number; fill the earth and subdue it. Rule over the fish of the sea and the birds of the air and over every living creature that moves on the ground" (Genesis 1:28).

David confirmed for all humanity the original great commission that God gave to Adam and Eve: "You gave them charge of everything you made, putting all things under their authority" (Psalm 8:6, NLT).

Mankind's reign on the earth is introduced in the first chapters of the Bible, mentioned throughout the Old Testament, discussed by Jesus in the Gospels and by Paul in the Epistles, and repeated by John in Revelation. From start to finish, we are told that our God-given purpose and destiny are to rule the earth.

God's desire is to prepare you now for what you will do forever. As any athlete, soldier, or farmer will tell you, preparation isn't always easy. But it's necessary, and its payoffs are huge. Our role as Kingdom rulers is not automatic—God makes it dependent on our faithful service here and now.

Are you ready to rule the New Earth? No? That's all right. God's plan is to shape your life to *make you ready*.

Are you cooperating with his plan, submitting to his training, and learning to call upon his strength and wisdom?

Thank you, Lord, that as your image bearers, we are still capable of bringing you glory, even in a world that is so bent. Thank you that your purpose and calling for us have not changed. Thank you that you are preparing a world for us to rule—and you are preparing us to rule it, for your eternal glory. Help us, Lord, never to think we do not have a role in your plan for our lives. Help us to fulfill our responsibilities and exercise the spiritual disciplines of meditation, prayer, fasting, giving, and serving others, so that we might be the sorts of children and servants that you take pleasure in commending and rewarding.

DAY 27

A GOVERNMENT WE'LL LOVE TO BE A PART OF

I confer on you a kingdom, just as my Father conferred one on me, so that you may eat and drink at my table in my kingdom and sit on thrones, judging the twelve tribes of Israel. — LUKE 22:29-30

A place in God's creative order has been reserved for each one of us from before the beginnings of cosmic existence. His plan is for us to develop, as apprentices to Jesus, to the point where we can take our place in the ongoing creativity of the universe.[57]
 — DALLAS WILLARD

The Bible's central story line revolves around a question: Who will reign over the earth? Earth's destiny hangs in the balance. Because it is the realm where God's glory has been the most challenged and resisted, it is also the stage on which his glory will be the most graphically demonstrated. By reclaiming, restoring, renewing, and resurrecting Earth—and empowering a regenerated mankind to reign over it—God will accomplish his purpose of bringing glory to himself.

Righteous human beings, first enthroned by God to reign over the earth from Eden, then dethroned by their own sin and Satan, will be re-enthroned with God forever. "And they will reign for ever and ever" (Revelation 22:5).

Upon hearing for the first time that mankind will rule the earth, govern cities, and reign forever, countless people have told me they're uncomfortable with the idea. It sounds presumptuous and self-important. If it were *our* idea to reign over the universe, it would indeed be presumptuous, even blasphemous. But it was *not* our idea, it was God's. And it's not a minor or peripheral doctrine; it's at the very heart of Scripture.

God's purpose and plan will not fully be achieved until Christ confers on us the Kingdom he has won. This will take place after our bodily resurrection, when we will eat and drink with the resurrected Christ on the resurrected Earth. Jesus said, "I confer on you a kingdom, just as my Father conferred one on me, so that you may eat and drink at my table in my kingdom and sit on thrones, judging the twelve tribes of Israel" (Luke 22:29-30).

This is an astounding statement, one that should cause us to pause in wonder. Christ is conferring to us a kingdom? A *kingdom*? To us? The apostles will rule most prominently, but Scripture makes it clear that Christ will make rulers of everyone who serves him humbly and faithfully here and now:

"His master replied, 'Well done, good and faithful servant! You have been faithful with a few things; I will put you in charge of many things'" (Matthew 25:21).

"If we endure, we will also reign with him" (2 Timothy 2:12). As Christians, we've been born into the family of an incredibly wealthy landowner. Our Father has a family business that stretches across the entire universe. He will entrust management of this business to us, his heirs, and that's what we'll do for eternity: manage God's assets and rule his universe, representing him as his children, his image-bearers, and his ambassadors.

Still, a number of people have said to me, "But I don't *want* to rule. That's not my idea of Heaven."

Well, it's *God's* idea of Heaven. Whose idea do you think is better, yours or his? We are part of God's family, and it's a royal family, because he's the King. Ruling the universe is the family business. To want no part of ruling the Kingdom is to want no part of our Father. It may sound spiritual to say we don't want to rule, but because God is the one who wants us to rule, the truly spiritual response is to be interested in and embrace his plans and purposes.

Whom will we rule? Other people. Angels. If God wishes, he could even create new beings for us to rule. Who will rule over us? Other people. That may go against the grain of our values and assumptions that in Heaven everything will be equal for everyone, but it is nonetheless true.

There will be a social hierarchy of government, but there's no indication of a *relational* hierarchy. There will be no pride, envy, boasting, elitism, or anything else sinful. The differences in our responsibilities will be a manifestation of God's creativity, as well as a reward for our faithful service here and now. As we're different in race, nationality, gender, personality, gifting, and passions, so we'll be different in positions of service. Scripture teaches that God will evaluate our service for him on Earth to determine how we'll serve him on the New Earth. The humble servant will be put in charge of much, whereas the one who has lorded it over others in the present world will have power taken away: "Everyone who exalts himself will be humbled, and he who humbles himself will be exalted" (Luke 14:11). If we serve faithfully on the present Earth, God will give us permanent management positions on the New Earth: "Whoever can be trusted with very little can also be trusted with much" (Luke 16:10).

We've been conditioned to associate governing with self-promoting arrogance, corruption, inequality, and inefficiency. But these are perversions, not inherent properties of leadership. Imagine responsibility, service, and leadership that are pure joy. Of course, not all positions of responsibility involve people. Adam and Eve governed animals before there were any other people. Some of us may be granted the privilege of caring for animals. Perhaps some will care for forests. Ruling will likely involve the management of all God's creation, not just people.

Perhaps God will offer us a choice, in keeping with our service for him on Earth, of where we might want to serve him on the New Earth. In any case, we can be certain that we'll do something we enjoy, because on the New Earth we'll want what God wants.

In addition, we'll have no more skepticism and disillusionment about government. Why? Because we'll be governed by Christlike rulers, and all of us will be under the grand and gracious government of Christ himself. We will forever rejoice that "of the increase of his government and peace there will be no end" (Isaiah 9:7).

Does this sound like a government you'd like to be part of?

Father, thank you that a perfect government awaits us, one for which we will always be thankful and one for which we will always be proud. Though we may be patriotic and proud citizens of our present earthly nations, remind us that our true citizenship is in Heaven. Remind us that one day we will live on a truly united planet where all nations will share a total devotion and allegiance to Jesus, King of kings and Lord of lords. God, empower us to unashamedly affirm our allegiance to you today, in our homes and workplaces and schools and neighborhoods. May you find us faithful, and may we one day hear you say those amazing words: "Well done, good and faithful servant. . . . Enter into the joy of your master."[58]

DAY 28

WHERE BELLMEN AND CLEANING LADIES WILL RULE

To him who overcomes, I will give the right to sit with me on my throne, just as I overcame and sat down with my Father on his throne. — REVELATION 3:21

If Baltimore or Liverpool were turned over to me, with power to do what I want with it, how would things turn out? An honest answer to this question might do much to prepare us for our eternal future in this universe.[59] — DALLAS WILLARD

When I speak to people about Heaven, they're often amazed to hear that we will reign for eternity over cities, nations, and territories. Many are skeptical. They think it sounds fanciful or just plain *wrong*.

Nothing demonstrates how far we've strayed from our understanding of biblical truth like our lack of knowledge about our destiny to rule the earth. Why are we so surprised about something that is spoken of throughout Scripture? Part of the reason may be that we've failed to understand key passages—even passages we are familiar with, including some we've memorized. For instance, are you aware that, along with thrones, crowns are the primary biblical symbol of ruling? Thus every mention of crowns as rewards speaks of our destiny to rule with Christ. Consider the following examples from one small portion of Scripture, Revelation 2–5. Note the references to crowns, thrones, and reigning:

"Be faithful, even to the point of death, and I will give you the crown of life" (2:10).

"To him who overcomes and does my will to the end, I will give authority over the nations" (2:26).

"I am coming soon. Hold on to what you have, so that no one will take your crown" (3:11).

"To him who overcomes, I will give the right to sit with me on my throne, just as I overcame and sat down with my Father on his throne" (3:21).

"The twenty-four elders fall down before him who sits on the throne. . . . They lay their crowns before the throne" (4:10).

"Your blood has ransomed people for God from every tribe and language and people and nation. And you have caused them to become a Kingdom of priests for our God. And they will reign on the earth" (5:9-10, NLT).

Who does God say will reign? Representatives of every tribe and language and people and nation. Where will they reign? On Earth, where people were made to dwell. Where on Earth? Likely with people of their own tribe, language, and nation, because Scripture explicitly tells us that national distinctives will still exist on the New Earth (Revelation 21:24, 26; 22:2).

Those coming out of the Great Tribulation will be rewarded by being given a special place "before the throne of God," where they will "serve him day and night" (Revelation 7:14-15). Notice that the Master rewards his faithful servants not by taking away responsibilities but by giving them greater ones.

Service is a reward, not a punishment. This idea is foreign to people who dislike their work and are only putting up with it until retirement. Some think that faithful work should be rewarded by a vacation for the rest of our lives. But God offers us something different: more work, more responsibilities, and increased opportunities along with greater abilities, resources, wisdom, and empowerment (sharp minds, strong bodies, clear purpose, and unabated joy). The more we serve Christ now, the greater our capacity will be to serve him in Heaven.

Will everyone be given the opportunity to rule in the new universe? Paul said that eternal rewards are available "not only to me, but also to all who have longed for his appearing" (2 Timothy 4:8). The word *all* is encouraging. If we are devoted to him, he will reward us.

"The Lord will reward everyone for whatever good he does, whether he is slave or free" (Ephesians 6:8). The word *everyone* is again encouraging. It won't be just a select few who are rewarded.

Whether putting us in charge of much or of little, God will reward us graciously and justly.

Should we be excited that God will reward us by making us rulers in his Kingdom? Absolutely. Jesus said, "Rejoice and be glad, because great is your reward in heaven" (Matthew 5:12).

God will choose who reigns as kings, and I'm confident some great surprises are in store for us. Christ gives us clues in Scripture as to the type of person he will choose: "Blessed are the poor in spirit, for theirs is the kingdom of heaven. . . . Blessed are the meek, for they will inherit the earth. . . . Blessed are those who are persecuted because of righteousness, for theirs is the kingdom of heaven" (Matthew 5:3, 5, 10). Also, "'God opposes the proud but gives grace to the humble.' Humble yourselves, therefore, under God's mighty hand, that he may lift you up in due time" (1 Peter 5:5-6).

Look around you to see the meek and the humble. They may include street sweepers, locksmiths' assistants, bus drivers, and stay-at-home moms who spend their days changing diapers, doing laundry, packing lunches, drying tears, and driving carpools.

I once gave one of my books to a delightful hotel bellman in Atlanta. I discovered he was a committed Christian. He said he'd been praying for our writers group, which was holding a conference at the hotel. Later, I gave him a little gift. He seemed stunned, overwhelmed. With tears in his eyes he said, "You didn't need to do that. I'm only a bellman." The moment he said those words, it struck me that this brother had spent his life serving other people. It will likely be someone like him that I'll have the privilege of serving under in God's Kingdom. He was "only a bellman" who spoke with warmth and love, who served, who quietly prayed in the background for the success of a Christian writers conference in his hotel, his place of service. I saw Jesus in that bellman, and there was no "only" about him.

Who will be the kings of the New Earth? I think that bellman will be one of them. And I will consider it an honor to carry his bags.

Keep your eyes open today to those around you, and ask yourself, which of these people might one day be kings and queens of the New Earth?

☨ *Lord, thank you that we can catch glimpses of your servant leadership in those we see around us, often those whom society would consider "beneath" us. Thank you that we will have the privilege of serving under people who have proven themselves in this life by serving you and others with humility and grace. What a joy it will be to serve you as we serve under them.*

DAY 29

THE NEW EARTH: A GREATER EDEN

The desert shall rejoice and blossom as the rose.
— Isaiah 35:1, NKJV

In the truest sense, Christian pilgrims have the best of both worlds. We have joy whenever this world reminds us of the next, and we take solace whenever it does not.
— Randy Alcorn

To catch a glimpse of Heaven, we don't need to take a metaphysical journey. We need only to take a close look at Earth and imagine what it once was—and therefore what it will one day be again. We can also take a close look at people, including ourselves, and imagine who *mankind* once was—and who we will one day be.

The present Earth, with all its natural wonders, gives us a foretaste and a glimpse of what the New Earth will be like without the desecration of the Fall. People, including ourselves, give us a foretaste and a glimpse of what mankind will be like on the New Earth without the corruption of sin. Our lives, including our society and culture, give us a foretaste and a glimpse of what the next life will be without the contamination of sin.

Every earthly joy—including the joy of reunion—is an inkling, a whisper of greater joy. The Grand Canyon, the Alps, the Amazon rain forests, the Serengeti Plain—these are rough sketches of the New Earth.

All our lives we've been dreaming of the New Earth. Whenever we see beauty in water, wind, flower, deer, man, woman, or child, we catch a glimpse of Heaven. Like Eden, the New Earth will be a place of sensory delight, breathtaking beauty, satisfying relationships, and personal joy.

As Eden is our backward-looking reference point, the New Earth is our forward-looking reference point. We should expect the New Earth to be like Eden, only better. And that's exactly what Scripture promises:

"Indeed, the LORD will comfort Zion; He will comfort all her waste places and her wilderness He will make like Eden, and her desert like the garden of the LORD; joy and gladness will be found in her, thanksgiving and sound of a melody" (Isaiah 51:3, NASB).

"They will say, 'This desolate land has become like the garden of Eden; and the waste, desolate and ruined cities are fortified and inhabited'" (Ezekiel 36:35, NASB).

"Instead of the thorn shall come up the cypress tree, and instead of the brier shall come up the myrtle tree" (Isaiah 55:13, NKJV).

We've never seen men and women as they were intended to be. We've never seen animals in their pre-Fall existence. We see only marred remnants of what once was. Likewise, we've never seen nature unchained and undiminished. We've seen it only cursed and decaying. Yet even now we see a great deal that pleases and excites us, much that moves our hearts to worship.

If the underside of Heaven, the back of the tapestry, so to speak, can be so beautiful, what does the front side look like? If the devastated remains of a cursed Earth are still so stunning, what will Earth look like when it is restored, and even enhanced, to something far greater?

C. S. Lewis and J. R. R. Tolkien saw core truths in the old mythologies. In their books, they give us glimpses of people and beasts and trees that are vibrantly alive. As Lewis and Tolkien realized, "Pagan fables of paradise were dim and distorted recollections of Eden."[60]

In *The Last Battle*, C. S. Lewis portrays young Lucy as she mourns the loss of Narnia, a cherished world that she assumed had been forever destroyed. Jewel, the Unicorn, mourns too, calling his beloved Narnia, "The only world I've ever known."

Although Lucy and her family and friends are on the threshold of Aslan's country (Heaven), they still look back at Narnia and feel a profound loss:

> Suddenly Farsight the Eagle . . . alighted on the ground. . . .
> "Kings and Queens," he cried, "we have all been blind. . . . Narnia is not dead. This is Narnia."
> "But how can it be?" said Peter.

"Yes," said Eustace. . . . "We saw it all destroyed and the sun put out."

"And it's all so different," said Lucy.

"The Eagle is right," said the Lord Digory. "Listen, Peter. When Aslan said you could never go back to Narnia, he meant the Narnia you were thinking of. But that was not the real Narnia. That had a beginning and an end. It was only a shadow or a copy of the real Narnia, which has always been here and always will be here: just as our own world, England and all, is only a shadow or copy of something in Aslan's real world. You need not mourn over Narnia, Lucy. All of the old Narnia that mattered, all the dear creatures, have been drawn into the real Narnia through the Door. And of course it is different; as different as a real thing is from a shadow or as waking life is from a dream. . . ."

The difference between the old Narnia and the new Narnia was like that. The new one was a deeper country: every rock and flower and blade of grass looked as if it meant more. I can't describe it any better than that: if you ever get there, you will know what I mean.

It was the Unicorn who summed up what everyone was feeling. He stamped his right fore-hoof on the ground and neighed and then cried:

"I have come home at last! This is my real country! I belong here. This is the land I have been looking for all my life, though I never knew it till now. The reason why we loved the old Narnia is that it sometimes looked a little like this."[61]

Lewis captured the biblical theology of the old and New Earth, and the continuity between them, better than any theologian I've read. Did you catch his message? Our world is a Shadowlands, a copy of something that once was (Eden) and yet will be (the New Earth). All of the old Earth that matters will be drawn into Heaven.

Based on what Scripture tells us, I think that what Lewis envisioned is possible, even likely. On the New Earth we will see the *real* Earth, which includes the good things of God's natural creation and of man's creative expression to God's glory. On the New Earth, no good thing will be destroyed.

What are some of the good things from this world and from your own life that God might carry over to the New Earth?

⵰ *Father, we rejoice in your promise that you will restore the best of Eden to this suffering planet. Thank you that you will comfort Zion, and comfort all her waste places. Thank you that you will make her wilderness like Eden and her desert like the Garden of the Lord. Thank you that "joy and gladness will be found in her, thanksgiving and the sound of singing."[62] How great it will be to hear your people say, "This desolate land has become like the garden of Eden."[63] We will rejoice to see that day. Help us to rejoice today as we anticipate it.*

ANIMALS ON THE NEW EARTH?

I now establish my covenant with you and with your descendants after you and with every living creature that was with you—the birds, the livestock and all the wild animals, all those that came out of the ark with you— every living creature on earth. — GENESIS 9:9-10

The whole brute creation will then, undoubtedly, be restored, not only to the vigour, strength, and swiftness which they had at their creation, but to a far higher degree of each than they ever enjoyed.[64] — JOHN WESLEY

Isaiah 11:6-9 speaks of a coming glorious era on Earth:

The wolf will live with the lamb, the leopard will lie down with the goat, the calf and the lion and the yearling together; and a little child will lead them. The cow will feed with the bear, their young will lie down together, and the lion will eat straw like the ox. The infant will play near the hole of the cobra, and the young child put his hand into the viper's nest. They will neither harm nor destroy on all my holy mountain, for the earth will be full of the knowledge of the LORD as the waters cover the sea.

Some interpreters restrict this passage to the Millennium, but Isaiah anticipates an *eternal* Kingdom of God on Earth. Isaiah 65:17 and 66:22 specifically refer to the New Earth. Sandwiched in between, in Isaiah 65:25, is a reference very similar to that in Isaiah 11: "'The wolf and the lamb will feed together, and the lion will eat straw like the ox. . . . They will neither harm nor destroy on all my holy mountain,' says the LORD."

When will there be *no more harm* on the earth? Not on the old Earth. Not even during the Millennium, which will end in rebellion, warfare, judgment, and death. Only on the New Earth will there be *no more harm*. Indeed, God tells us, there will be no more death, mourning, or pain there (Revelation 21:4). These descriptions of animals peacefully inhabiting the earth *may* have application to a millennial kingdom on the old Earth, but their primary reference point seems to be God's eternal Kingdom, where men and animals will together enjoy a redeemed Earth.

What was God's original design for the earth? We need not wonder: "God made the wild animals according to their kinds, the livestock according to their kinds, and all the creatures that move along the ground according to their kinds. And God saw that it was good" (Genesis 1:25).

"Now the LORD God had formed out of the ground all the beasts of the field and all the birds of the air" (Genesis 2:19). Only humans and animals were formed from the ground. God handmade them, linking them to the earth and to each other.

When God breathed a spirit into Adam's body, which was

made from the earth, Adam became *nephesh*, a "living being" (Genesis 2:7). Remarkably, the same word, *nephesh*, is used for animals, just as it is for people—*both* are given God's breath of life (Genesis 1:30; 2:7; 6:17; 7:15, 22). The word *nephesh* is often translated "living being" or "soul." *Nephesh* includes the animating principle that God puts into animal and human bodies.

Don't misunderstand. Humans and animals are very different, and *in no sense are they equal.* The point is simply that we *do* share certain significant similarities as living beings created by God. The immaterial being of humans continues to survive after death, whereas animals may not. (Of course, this wouldn't prevent God from re-creating the animals if he wants to.) However, to do justice to Scripture, we need to recognize that people and animals are both said to be unique, living beings. The fact that God has a future plan for both mankind and the earth strongly suggests that he also has a future plan for animals. God's words to Noah regarding the first "new earth" (post-Flood) support this idea:

"You are to bring into the ark two of all living creatures, male and female, to keep them alive with you. Two of every kind of bird, of every kind of animal and of every kind of creature that moves along the ground will come to you to be kept alive" (Genesis 6:19-20).

Animals were given as companions and helpers to mankind, and humans were to rule the animals benevolently. God not only preserved animals from the Flood, he also, remarkably, included them in his new covenant. Notice the repeated emphasis on animals:

"I now establish my covenant with you and with your descendants after you and *with every living creature* that was with you—*the birds, the livestock and all the wild animals*, all those that came out of the ark with you—*every living creature* on earth. . . . Never again will there be a flood to destroy the earth. . . ."

And God said, "This is the sign of the covenant I am making between me and you and *every living creature* with you, a covenant for all generations to come. . . . I will remember my covenant between me and you and *all living creatures of every kind.* . . . Whenever the rainbow appears in the clouds, I will see it and remember the everlasting covenant between God and *all living creatures of every kind* on the earth. . . ."

God said to Noah, "This is the sign of the covenant I have established between me and all life on the earth." (Genesis 9:9-17, emphasis added)

God's plan for a renewed Earth after the Flood emphatically involved animals. Wouldn't we likewise expect his plan for a renewed Earth after the future judgment to include animals?

Second Peter 3:5-7 draws a direct parallel between God's past judgment of the earth with water and his future judgment with fire. Mankind was judged in the Flood, but *God didn't limit his rescue to people*; he also rescued representatives of every animal species to populate the earth. This is a powerful picture of what Romans 8 states: mankind and animals and all creation are linked together not only in curse and judgment but also in blessing and deliverance. Shouldn't we expect the same in the coming judgment by fire?

Since we know God will fashion the New Earth with renewed people and renewed features of ground and water and trees and fruit, shouldn't we expect him also to include renewed animals?

The burden of proof falls not on the assumption that animals *will* be part of God's New Earth, but on the assumption that they *won't*. Would God withhold from us on the New Earth what he gave to Adam and Eve in Eden for delight, companionship, and help? Would he revoke his decision to put animals on Earth with people, placing them under our care and rule? Or will he follow through on his original design?

Look around today at the animals you come across. Ask yourself, why does the Creator consider these creatures important enough to include them in his original creation and his covenant promise?

⇌ *Lord, the extent of your redemptive plan boggles our minds. Preserve us from our narrow thinking, which is so quick to limit and restrict the scope of your redemption. You repeatedly emphasized that your covenant was not just with humans but with animals as well. Open our eyes to see the nature of your creative work in animals, and their essential connection to the earth and to us. Help us to anticipate living on the New Earth and beholding in your creatures your attributes and delights, in greater ways than ever before.*

DAY 31

ANIMALS WE LOVE MIGHT LIVE AGAIN

The creation itself will be liberated from its bondage to decay and brought into the glorious freedom of the children of God. We know that the whole creation has been groaning as in the pains of childbirth.... We ourselves ... groan inwardly as we wait eagerly for ... the redemption of our bodies. — ROMANS 8:21-23

Something better remains after death for these poor creatures. ... [They] shall one day be delivered from this bondage of corruption, and shall then receive an ample amends for all their present sufferings.[65] — JOHN WESLEY

Humorist Will Rogers said, "If there are no dogs in heaven, then when I die I want to go where they went." This statement was, of course, based on sentiment, not theology, but it reflects something biblical: a God-given affection for animals.

I've often thanked God for my golden retriever, who crawled into my sleeping bag as I lay in my backyard gazing up at the stars when I was a boy. Though I didn't know God then, he touched my life through that dog. Nanci and I have experienced many hours of laughter and joy with animals. When our children and grandchildren have delighted in animals, they have delighted in God, their Creator.

Christ proclaims from his throne on the New Earth: "Behold, I am making all things new" (Revelation 21:5, NASB). It's not just people who will be renewed, but the earth and everything in it. Do "all things" include animals? Of course. Horses, cats, dogs, deer, dolphins, and squirrels—as well as the inanimate creation—will be beneficiaries of Christ's death and resurrection. Christ's emphasis isn't on making new things, but on making old things new. It's not about inventing the unfamiliar, but restoring and enhancing the familiar. Jesus seems to be saying, "I'll take all I made the first time, including people and nature and animals and the earth itself, and bring them back as new, fresh, and indestructible."

Romans 8:21-23 is a clear statement that our resurrection, the redemption of our bodies, will bring deliverance not only to us *but also to the rest of creation, which has been groaning in its suffering*. This raises an obvious question: Who or what in this creation, besides human beings, is groaning in suffering and is waiting for deliverance? Surely the most obvious answer is *animals*. This seems to indicate that on the New Earth, after mankind's resurrection, some animals who once suffered will join God's children in glorious freedom from death and decay.

If God created on the New Earth human beings who had never before existed—rather than resurrecting people who had lived on the old Earth—would it fulfill the promise in Romans 8 of redemption, deliverance, and resurrection? No. Why? For the passage to be fulfilled, those redeemed and resurrected into the new world *must be the same people who suffered in the old world.* Otherwise, their longing for redemption would go unmet.

As mankind goes, so go the animals. If we take to its logical conclusion the parallel that Paul makes between humans and animals groaning, then *at least some of those animals who suffered on the old Earth must be made whole on the New Earth.*

Remember, it's not some abstract "animalkind" that cries out; it's specific animals living and suffering and dying on the old Earth, just as it's specific, suffering people who groan and cry out for their own resurrection—not for someone else's. This suggests that God may resurrect, or at least re-create, certain animals that lived on the old Earth.

If God indeed will re-create some animals from the old Earth on the new, it seems reasonable to ask whether our beloved pets might be included.

While speaking at a Bible college, I asked the audience to raise their hands if God had deeply touched their lives through particular animals they'd had as pets. Ninety percent of the thousand or more people raised their hands.

Animals aren't nearly as valuable as people, but God is still their Maker and has affected many people's lives through them. It would be simple for him to re-create a pet on the New Earth if he wanted to. He's the *giver* of all good gifts, not a *taker*. And, as a parent, he is far better at giving good gifts to his children than we are (Matthew 7:9-11). Certainly, if it would make us happier in Heaven, God would be willing to restore a favorite animal to us, for by finding happiness in God's creation, we find our happiness in him.

God could do one of three things regarding animals on the

New Earth. He could (1) create entirely new animals; (2) bring animals back to life that have suffered in our present world, giving them immortal bodies (this could be through re-creation, not necessarily through resurrection); or (3) create some brand-new animals "from scratch" *and* bring some old ones back to life.

We must be careful to avoid theological error. We should recognize and affirm the fundamental differences between humans and animals. That's why I avoid using the term *resurrection* with respect to animals on the New Earth. However, in a broad sense, both *redemption* and *resurrection* can appropriately apply not only to mankind but also to the earth, vegetation, and animals. Of course, a resurrected field, meadow, flower, or animal would in no sense be equal to a resurrected human; it's simply that redemption and resurrection can ride the coattails of mankind, just as the consequences of the Fall did.

In *The Great Divorce*, C. S. Lewis portrays Sarah Smith as an ordinary woman on Earth who became a great woman in Heaven. On Earth, she loved both people and animals. In Heaven, she's surrounded by the very animals she cared for on Earth. Could that actually happen? Knowing our gracious God and the delights he lavishes upon his beloved children and even his beloved animals, I would not be surprised.

Have you ever had a pet that God used in your life? Has God reminded you of any of his attributes through animals? Do you want to thank God for touching your life through animals?

Father, thank you for the roles that various animals have played in our lives, from childhood on. Thank you that you are so aware of your creation that no bird falls to the ground without your notice. Thank you for building provisions for animals into your law, including a day of rest from labor. Clearly your heart is touched by all your creatures, great and small. Lord, thanks for promising that the rest of creation, not just humans, will be delivered from suffering at our resurrection to enjoy your new world. If it happens to be part of your plan to bring animals from this old Earth to the New Earth, including our pets, we will thank you for them, even as we thank you now for the comfort and companionship and entertainment you have provided us through them.

DAY 32

THE NEW JERUSALEM

[I saw] the river of the water of life, as clear as crystal, flowing from the throne of God and of the Lamb down the middle of the great street of the city.

— REVELATION 22:1-2

I am groaning with inexpressible groaning on my wanderer's path, and remembering Jerusalem with my heart lifted up towards it—Jerusalem my homeland, Jerusalem my mother.[66]

— AUGUSTINE

Why did the great explorers, such as Columbus, Magellan, and their crews, seek after "the new world"? Because they were sinners? No. Because as humans *we were made to seek out new worlds.* God created us to be seekers and explorers and rulers of the earth. (The fact that human sin tainted the actions of many explorers should not cause us to lose sight of this.)

The demands and distractions of our present lives often cause us to set aside or stifle our longings to explore, yet they still surface. On the New Earth, those desires won't be thwarted by pragmatic considerations. Rather, they will be stimulated and encouraged.

And they will never be twisted or diminished by sin, because there will be no sin. As we explore God's creation in the ages to come, eager to know him better through what we discover, we'll grow in our knowledge of him, becoming even more motivated to worship him for his wonders.

The first place we may wish to explore will be the largest city that has ever existed—the New Earth's capital city. The Bible says that the New Jerusalem will be a place of extravagant beauty and natural wonders—a vast Eden, integrated with the best of human culture, under the reign of Christ. More wealth than has been accumulated in all human history will be spread freely across this immense city.

The city's dimensions will be the equivalent of 1,400 miles (2,200 kilometers) in length, width, and height (Revelation 21:15-16). If a metropolis of this size were situated in the middle of North America, it would stretch from Canada to Mexico and from the Sierra Nevada to the Appalachians. Particularly because of its stated height, people debate whether these are literal or figurative measurements, but clearly we are to envision it as a city immense beyond imagination. Those concerned about crowded conditions have nothing to worry about.

Presumably, there will be many other cities on the New Earth, such as those Jesus mentions in the stewardship parables, where he says that in the Kingdom some will rule over five cities and some over ten (Luke 19:17, 19). The kings of nations who bring their treasures into the New Jerusalem must come from and return to somewhere. Presumably, they will come from other settlements beyond the New Jerusalem. But there will be no city like this one—for it will be home to the King of kings.

Heaven's capital city will be filled with visual magnificence. "It shone with the glory of God, and its brilliance was like that of a very precious jewel, like a jasper, clear as crystal" (Revelation 21:11). John describes the opulence: "The wall was made of jasper, and the city of pure gold, as pure as glass. The foundations of the city walls were decorated with every kind of precious stone" (Revelation 21:18-19). John then names twelve stones, eight of which correspond to the stones of the high priest's breastplate (Exodus 28–29).

"The twelve gates were twelve pearls, each gate made of a single pearl. The great street of the city was of pure gold, like transparent glass" (Revelation 21:21). The precious stones and gold represent incredible wealth, suggestive of the exorbitant riches of God's splendor.

John also describes a natural wonder in the center of the New Jerusalem: "The river of the water of life, as clear as crystal, flowing from the throne of God and of the Lamb down the middle of the great street of the city" (Revelation 22:1-2). Why is water important? Because the city is a center of human life and water is an essential part of life. Ghosts don't need water, but human bodies do. We all know what it's like to be thirsty, but John was writing to people who lived in a bone-dry climate, who would have grasped the wonder of constantly available fresh water, pure and uncontaminated, able to satisfy the deepest thirst.

On the New Earth, we won't have to leave the city to find natural beauty. It will be incorporated into the city, with the river of life at its center. The river flows down the main street, most likely splitting into countless smaller streams that flow throughout the rest of the city. Can you picture people talking and laughing beside this river, sticking their hands and faces into the water and drinking?

After John describes the river of life, he mentions another striking feature: "On each side of the river stood the tree of life, bearing twelve crops of fruit, yielding its fruit every month. And the leaves of the tree are for the healing of the nations" (Revelation 22:2). It appears human beings may draw their strength and vitality through eating of this tree. The tree will produce not one crop but twelve. The newness and freshness of Heaven is demonstrated in the monthly yield of fruit. The fruit is not merely to be admired but consumed: "To him who overcomes, I will grant to eat of the tree of life which is in the Paradise of God" (Revelation 2:7, NASB).

What kind of a view will we have in this city? We know that the New Earth will have at least one mountain, "a mountain great and high" (Revelation 21:10), and we can assume it has hundreds or thousands of them. We may stand on a wall of the great city and look out at breathtaking horizons inviting us to come explore God's New Earth.

And what will we find if we leave the city? The New Earth's waterfalls may dwarf Niagara—or the New Niagara Falls may dwarf the one we know now. We'll find rock formations more spectacular than Yosemite's, peaks that overshadow the Himalayas, and forests deeper and richer than anything we see in my beloved Pacific Northwest. It's likely that our tastes will differ enough that some of us, at various times, will prefer to gather for great cultural events, while others will want to withdraw to feed ducks on a lake, and still others will leave the city with their companions to pursue adventures in some undeveloped place. But wherever we go and whatever we do, we'll never leave the presence of the King. For though he will dwell centrally in the New Jerusalem, he will also be fully present to the ends of the earth and in the far reaches of the new universe.

What do you not like about city life that you're glad won't be in the New Jerusalem? What do you love about city life—redeemed city life—that you look forward to in the great city?

Father, thank you for the great city that awaits us, a city that will contain all that is good about cities and nothing that's bad. Thanks that we will not have to say farewell to all the good aspects of city life—to the beautiful architecture and cultural expressions, the gatherings, and perhaps great restaurants as well. Thank you, too, that both inside and outside the city we will see natural wonders that proclaim your glory. We are grateful that at death we will not say a permanent good-bye to the creation that declares your majesty. Rather, we will be brought back to a physical universe redeemed and cleansed of all that now threatens to obscure you and your greatness. How amazing it will be to eat the fruit of the tree of life in the midst of the city. Help us to face today, Lord, in light of the marvelous day that is coming.

DAY 33

BEING OURSELVES IN HEAVEN

Many will come from the east and the west, and will take their places at the feast with Abraham, Isaac and Jacob in the kingdom of heaven. — MATTHEW 8:11

Until you have given up your self to Him you will not have a real self.[67] — C. S. LEWIS

In Dickens's *A Christmas Carol*, Ebenezer Scrooge was terrified when he saw a phantom.

"Who are you?" Scrooge asked.

"Ask me who I *was*," the ghost replied.

"Who were you then?" said Scrooge.

"In life I was your partner, Jacob Marley."

In Stanley Kubrick's movie *2010*, Dave Bowman appears in ghostly form. When asked who he is, he replies, "I *was* David Bowman."

These are common portrayals of the afterlife, disembodied ghosts—pale reflections of a person's former self—floating in a nebulous netherworld. But these stories do not accurately reflect what our lives will be like on the New Earth. A central part of our bodily resurrection will be the continuity of our identity. If the eternal Heaven were a disembodied state, then our humanity would either be diminished or transcended, and we would never again be ourselves after we die.

Contrast Jacob Marley's ghost with Job, who said, "After my skin has been destroyed, yet in my flesh I will see God; I myself will see him with my own eyes—I, and not another" (Job 19:26-27).

Contrast the ghost that *was* Dave Bowman with the risen Jesus, who said, "Look at my hands and my feet. It is I myself! Touch me and see; a ghost does not have flesh and bones, as you see I have" (Luke 24:39).

Jesus called people by name in Heaven, including Lazarus in the present Heaven (Luke 16:25) and Abraham, Isaac, and Jacob in the future Heaven (Matthew 8:11). A name denotes a distinct identity, an individual. The fact that people in Heaven can be called by their earthly name demonstrates that they remain the same people—without the bad parts—forever.

You will be yourself in Heaven. *Who else would you be?*

If Bob, a man on Earth, is no longer Bob when he gets to Heaven, then Bob was not actually redeemed and Bob did not go to Heaven. When I arrive in Heaven, however changed I will be, if I'm not the same person I was on Earth—with the same identity, history, and memory—then *I* didn't go to Heaven.

If we aren't ourselves in the afterlife, then how can we be rewarded or held accountable for anything we did in this life? The Judgment would be meaningless. The doctrines of judgment and eternal rewards depend on people retaining their distinct identities from this life to the next.

In Buddhism, Hinduism, and New Age mysticism, individuality is obliterated or assimilated into Nirvana. But biblically, even though we may feel lost in God's immensity, we will find our identity when we see him. "Whoever loses his life for me will find it" (Matthew 16:25).

As our genetic code and fingerprints are unique now, we should expect the same in our new bodies. God is the Creator of individual identities and personalities. He makes no two snowflakes alike, much less two people. Not even "identical twins" are completely identical. Individuality preceded sin and the Curse. It's God's plan, and he receives greater glory through our differences.

Heaven's inhabitants don't simply rejoice over nameless multitudes coming to God. They rejoice over each and every person (Luke 15:4-7, 10). That's a powerful affirmation of Heaven's view of each person as an individual, whose life is observed and cared for.

When Moses and Elijah appeared out of Heaven at the Transfiguration, the disciples recognized them as the distinct individuals they were. When Jesus was resurrected, he didn't become someone else; he remained who he had been before his resurrection: "It is I myself!" In John's Gospel, Jesus deals with Mary, Thomas, and Peter in very personal ways, drawing on his previous knowledge of them. His relationships from his preresurrected state carried over. When Thomas said, "My Lord and my God" (John 20:28), he knew he was speaking to the same Jesus he'd followed. When John said, "It is the Lord" (John 21:7), he meant, "It's really him—the Jesus we have known."

"'As the new heavens and the new earth that I make will endure before me,' declares the LORD, 'so will your name and descendants endure'" (Isaiah 66:22). Our personal history and identity will endure from one Earth to the next. Jesus said that he would drink the fruit of the vine again, *with* his disciples, *in* his Father's kingdom (Matthew 26:28).

In Heaven, will we be called by our earthly names? When it says that the names of God's children are written in the Lamb's Book of Life (Revelation 20:15; 21:27), I believe those are our earthly names. God calls people in Heaven by their earthly names—Abraham, Isaac, and Jacob, for instance. Our names reflect our individuality. To have the same name written in Heaven that was ours on Earth speaks of the continuity between this life and the next.

In addition to our earthly names, we'll receive new names in Heaven (Isaiah 62:2; 65:15; Revelation 2:17; 3:12). But new names don't invalidate the old ones.

A man wrote me expressing his fear of losing his identity in Heaven: "Will being like Jesus mean the obliteration of self?" He was afraid that we'd all be alike, that he and his treasured friends would lose the distinguishing traits and eccentricities that make them special. But he needn't worry. We can all be like Jesus in character yet remain very different from one another in personality.

Distinctiveness is God's creation, not Satan's. What makes us unique will survive. In fact, much of our uniqueness may be uncovered for the first time. We'll be real people with real desires, but holy ones. We'll have real feelings, but feelings redeemed from pride and insecurity and wrong thinking. We'll be ourselves—with all the good and none of the bad. And we will consider it, in just the right sense, a privilege to be who God has made us to be.

Do you look forward to being yourself, without any of the things that get in the way of being the person God designed you to be? What steps can you take today to become more that person on this side of Heaven?

⇌ Lord, on the one hand, we want to be liberated from ourselves, freed from confusion and wrong motives, pride, self-centeredness, self-loathing, self-everything. Yet in saying that, what we mean is that we want to become the persons you intend for us to be. We want to be the unique image-bearers you've made us, and we also want to be like Jesus. We look forward to being ourselves without the bad parts, free at last to be who you have made us to be. Thank you that you have already redeemed us and given us a righteous nature in Christ. Help us to reckon ourselves dead to sin and alive to righteousness. Help us to live in a manner consistent with our new nature, growing in Christlikeness every day.

DAY 34

EATING AND DRINKING ON THE NEW EARTH

Blessed is the man who will eat at the feast in the kingdom of God. — LUKE 14:15

Are symbolic banquets and symbolic wine and symbolic rivers and trees somehow superior to real banquets and real wine and real rivers and trees in God's eternal plan? These things are just some of the excellent features of the perfection and final goodness of the physical creation that God has made.[68]
— WAYNE GRUDEM

Words for *eating*, *meals*, and *food* appear more than one thousand times in Scripture, and the word translated "feast" occurs another 187 times. Feasting involves celebration and fun. Great conversations, storytelling, relationship building, and laughter all happen around the table. The Jewish feasts, including Passover, are spiritual gatherings that draw attention directly to God, his greatness, and his redemptive purposes.

People who love each other like to eat meals together. Jesus said to his disciples, "I confer on you a kingdom, just as my Father conferred one on me, so that you may eat and drink at my table in my kingdom" (Luke 22:29-30).

Scripture says, "On this mountain the LORD Almighty will prepare a feast of rich food for all peoples, a banquet of aged wine—the best of meats and the finest of wines" (Isaiah 25:6).

The resurrected Jesus invited his disciples, "Come and have breakfast." He prepared them a meal, then ate bread and fish with them (John 21:4-14). He proved that resurrected bodies are capable of eating food, *real* food. Christ could have abstained from eating. The fact that he didn't is a powerful statement about the nature of his resurrected body—and by implication, ours. "The Lord Jesus Christ . . . will transform our lowly bodies so that they will be like his glorious body" (Philippians 3:20-21).

Other passages indicate that we'll eat at feasts with Christ in an earthly Kingdom. Jesus said to his disciples, "I tell you I will not drink again of the fruit of the vine until the kingdom of God comes" (Luke 22:18). Where will the Kingdom of God come? To Earth. Where will God's Kingdom reach its ultimate and eternal state? On the New Earth.

Jesus said that "many will come from the east and the west, and will take their places at the feast with Abraham, Isaac and Jacob in the kingdom of heaven" (Matthew 8:11).

An angel in Heaven said to John, "Blessed are those who are invited to the wedding supper of the Lamb!" (Revelation 19:9). What do people do at any supper—especially a wedding supper? Eat and drink. Talk, tell stories, celebrate, and laugh. Have dessert. Wedding feasts in the Middle East often lasted a full week. (And we won't only be guests—we'll be the bride!)

Part of the conclusive evidence for the true physical resurrection of Christ is the fact that he ate and drank with his disciples:

> When he had said this, he showed them his hands and feet. And while they still did not believe it because of joy and amazement, he asked them, "Do you have anything here to eat?" They gave him a piece of broiled fish, and he took it and ate it in their presence. (Luke 24:40-43)

> God raised him from the dead on the third day and caused him to be seen. He was not seen by all the people but by witnesses whom God had already chosen—by us who ate and drank with him after he rose from the dead. (Acts 10:39-41)

> Jesus said to them, "Bring some of the fish you have just caught. . . . Come and have breakfast." None of the disciples dared ask him, "Who are you?" They knew it was the Lord. Jesus came, took the bread and gave it to them, and did the same with the fish. This was now the third time Jesus appeared to his disciples after he was raised from the dead. . . .When they had finished eating . . . (John 21:10-15)

These passages emphatically link eating and drinking to the resurrected state. The fact that it's so often repeated means it's not viewed as incidental. Scripture goes out of its way to prevent us from embracing the very misconceptions so many of us have:

that life in Heaven will be "spiritual," not physical, and that we will not partake of any of the basic pleasures of this life.

Yet another biblical passage gives us insight about eating in Heaven. One day, while eating in the home of a Pharisee, Jesus said to his host, "When you give a luncheon or dinner, . . . invite the poor, the crippled, the lame, the blind, and you will be blessed. Although they cannot repay you, you will be repaid at the resurrection of the righteous" (Luke 14:12-14).

When Jesus made this reference to the resurrection of the righteous, a man at the same dinner said to him, "Blessed is the man who will eat at the feast in the kingdom of God" (Luke 14:15). Because they were eating together at the time, the man was obviously referring to literal eating and feasting. If he was mistaken about literally eating after the final Resurrection, Jesus had every opportunity to correct him. But he didn't. In fact, he built on the man's words to tell a story about someone who prepared a banquet and invited many guests (Luke 14:16-24). Clearly, both the man and Jesus were talking about literal eating at literal banquets, like the one they were attending.

I don't always take the Bible literally. Scripture contains many figures of speech. But just because the Bible uses some figures of speech in describing Heaven, it doesn't mean that everything the Bible says about Heaven is figurative. When we're told that we'll have resurrected bodies like Christ's and that he ate in his resurrected body, why should we assume he was speaking figuratively when he refers to tables, banquets, and eating and drinking in his Kingdom?

We're commanded, "Honor God in your body" (1 Corinthians 6:20, NASB). What will we do for eternity? Glorify God in our bodies. We're told, "Whether you eat or drink or whatever you do, do it all for the glory of God" (1 Corinthians 10:31). What will we do for eternity? Eat, drink, and do it all for the glory of God.

The food we eat is from God's hand. We can trust that the food we'll eat on the New Earth, some of it familiar and some of it brand new, will taste better than anything we've ever eaten here. We won't need fine meals in Heaven; we don't *need* them now, but we enjoy them now for the same reason we'll enjoy them then—because God made us to enjoy food and to glorify him as we eat and drink (1 Corinthians 10:31). God tells us that he "richly provides us with everything for our enjoyment" (1 Timothy 6:17).

On the New Earth, we will "drink . . . from the spring of the water of life" (Revelation 21:6). God will prepare for us "a banquet of aged wine . . . the finest of wines" (Isaiah 25:6). Not only will we drink water and wine, we'll eat from fruit trees (Revelation 22:2), and there's every reason to believe we'll drink juice made from the twelve fruits of the tree of life.

Along with water, wine, and fruit juice, is there any reason to suppose we won't drink coffee or tea in Heaven? Can you imagine having a cup of coffee or tea with Jesus on the New Earth? If you can't, why not?

Those who suffer from food allergies, weight problems, or addictions—and thus can't consume certain foods and drinks—may look forward to enjoying every good thing on the New Earth. To be liberated from sin, death, and bondage on the New Earth will not mean we'll enjoy *fewer* pleasures, but *more*. And the God who delights in our pleasures will be glorified in our grateful praise.

You and I have never eaten food in a world untouched by the Fall and the Curse. The best-tasting food we've ever eaten wasn't nearly as good as it must have tasted in Eden, or as it will on the New Earth.

Does your mouth water for the tastes and smells of food in the world to come? Do you think that God *wants* us to look forward to eating at his table and enjoying the bountiful foods and drinks he has in store for us?

☩ *Father, we've eaten many things in many places, but we've merely sampled the vast array of foods available on this present Earth. We may not have yet tasted our favorite food—and if we have, it has never tasted as good as it will in your coming Kingdom. Remind us that our best meals, our best conversations, our deepest laughter, and the most engaging stories are still ahead of us, to be experienced at feasts on the New Earth. Thank you, our kind and extravagant Father, that these things are not trivial and incidental; you not only created them for our pleasure in this world but promise them for our abundant lives in the far better world to come.*

DAY 35

KNOWING AND LEARNING

God raised us up with Christ and seated us with him in the heavenly realms in Christ Jesus, in order that in the coming ages he might show the incomparable riches of his grace. — EPHESIANS 2:6-7

How soon do earthly lovers come to an end of their discoveries of each other's beauty; how soon do they see all there is to be seen! But in Heaven there is eternal progress with new beauties always being discovered.[69] — JONATHAN EDWARDS

People often say, "We don't understand now, but in Heaven we'll know everything."

Is this true? Definitely not.

God alone is omniscient. When we die, we'll see things far more clearly, and we'll know much more than we do now, but we'll *never* know everything. (If we did, we'd be God!)

The apostle Paul writes, "Now we see but a poor reflection as in a mirror; then we shall see face to face. Now I know in part; then I shall know fully, even as I am fully known" (1 Corinthians 13:12).

To "know fully" doesn't mean that we'll be omniscient but that we will know without error and misconception. We'll "get it." We'll see God's face and therefore *truly* know him. But he will remain infinite and we will remain finite. We will know accurately, but not comprehensively.

In Heaven we'll be flawless, but not knowing everything isn't a flaw. It's just part of being finite. Angels don't know everything, and they long to know more (1 Peter 1:12). They're flawless, but finite. We should expect to long for greater knowledge, as angels do. And we'll spend eternity gaining the greater knowledge we seek.

One poll indicated that less than one in five people believe we will grow intellectually once we're in Heaven.[70] I heard a pastor say on the radio, "There will be no more learning in Heaven." One writer says that in Heaven, "Activities such as investigation, comprehending, and probing will never be necessary. Our understanding will be complete."[71]

But that's not what Scripture says.

Paul, in Ephesians 2:6-7, writes, "God raised us up with Christ and seated us with him in the heavenly realms in Christ Jesus, in order that in the coming ages he might show the incomparable riches of his grace." The word translated *show* means "to reveal." The phrase *in the coming ages* clearly indicates that this will be a progressive, ongoing revelation, in which we learn more and more about God's grace.

I often learn new things about my wife, daughters, and closest friends, even though I've known them for many years. If I can always be learning something new about finite, limited human beings, how much more will I be learning about Jesus in the ages to come? None of us will ever begin to exhaust his depths.

Jesus said to his disciples, "Learn from me" (Matthew 11:29). On the New Earth we'll have the privilege of sitting at Jesus' feet as Mary did, walking with him over the countryside as his disciples did, and always learning from him. In Heaven, we'll continually learn new things about God, going ever deeper in our understanding.

Occasionally we hear stories that provide a small taste of what we'll learn in eternity. One morning when I was speaking at a church, a young woman came up to me and said, "Do you remember a young man headed to college sitting next to you on a plane? You gave him your novel *Deadline*."

I give away a lot of my books on planes, but after some prompting, I remembered him. He was an unbeliever. We talked about Jesus, and I gave him the book and prayed for him as we got off the plane.

I was amazed when the young woman said, "He told me he never contacted you, so you wouldn't know what happened. He got to college, checked into the dorm, sat down, and read your book. When he was done, he confessed his sins and gave his life to Jesus. And I can honestly tell you, he's the most dynamic Christian I've ever met."

All I did was talk to a college student on an airplane, give him a book, and pray for him. But if the young woman hadn't told me what happened later, I wouldn't have had a clue. This made me think about how many great stories await us in Heaven, and how many we may not hear until we've been there a long time. We won't ever know everything, and even what we know, we won't know all at once. We'll be learners forever. Few things excite me more than that.

Jonathan Edwards maintained that we will continually become happier in Heaven in "a never-ending, ever-increasing discovery of more and more of God's glory with greater and greater joy in him." He said there will never be a time when there is "no more glory for the redeemed to discover and enjoy."

When we enter Heaven, we'll presumably begin with the knowledge we had at the time of death. God may enhance our knowledge and will correct countless wrong perceptions. I imagine he'll reveal many new things to us and then set us on a course of continual learning like that of Adam and Eve in the Garden. Perhaps angels or loved ones already in Heaven will be assigned to tutor us.

Think of what it will be like to discuss science with Isaac Newton, Michael Faraday, and Thomas Edison, or to discuss mathematics with Blaise Pascal. Imagine long talks with Malcolm Muggeridge or Francis Schaeffer. Think about discussing the writings of C. S. Lewis, J. R. R. Tolkien, G. K. Chesterton, or Dorothy Sayers with the authors themselves. How would you like to talk about the power of fiction at a roundtable with John Milton, Daniel Defoe, Victor Hugo, Fyodor Dostoyevsky, Leo Tolstoy, and Flannery O'Connor?

Imagine discussing the sermons of George Whitefield, Jonathan Edwards, Charles Finney, or Charles Spurgeon with the preachers themselves. Or talking about faith with George Mueller or Bill Bright and hearing their stories firsthand. You might cover the Civil War era with Abraham Lincoln and Harriet Beecher Stowe.

Or the history of missions with William Carey, Amy Carmichael, Lottie Moon, or Hudson and Maria Taylor.

Consider how exciting intellectual development will be. Father Boudreau writes, "The life of Heaven is one of intellectual pleasure. . . . There the intellect of man receives a supernatural light. . . . It is purified, strengthened, enlarged, and enabled to see God as He is in His very essence. It is enabled to contemplate, face to face, Him who is the first essential Truth. Who can fathom the exquisite pleasures of the human intellect when it thus sees all truth as it is in itself!"[72]

Imagine what Heaven will be like for those who never had the benefits of literacy and education. What joy they will have in drawing truths ever deeper and ever more from their God, the Well who will never run dry.

What have you always wanted to know that you may learn in Heaven? What are some things you'd like to study on the New Earth? How might your learning glorify God?

Father, thank you for your promise that in the ages to come you will be revealing the riches of your grace and kindness. We look forward to contemplating your person and works as we see your face. Remind us, Lord, that intellectual curiosity isn't part of the Curse—it is your blessing on us, your image-bearers. Thanks for making us with fertile, curious minds so that we might seek truth and find it in you, our greatest source of pleasure. Move us, Lord, not to wait until we die to study the great truths of your Word. Motivate us to turn off the television, draw away from the computer, set aside the endless housework, and open your Word. Draw us closer to you through great books that are saturated with your Word, and that show you as you really are.

DAY 36

RESTING AND WORKING

Blessed are the dead who die in the Lord from now on.... They will rest from their labor, for their deeds will follow them.... The throne of God and of the Lamb will be in the city, and his servants will serve him.
— REVELATION 14:13; 22:3

If there be so certain and glorious a rest for the saints, why is there no more industrious seeking after it? One would think, if a man did but once hear of such unspeakable glory to be obtained, and believed what he heard to be true, he should be transported with the vehemency of his desire after it, and should almost forget to eat and drink, and should care for nothing else, and speak of and inquire after nothing else, but how to get this treasure.[73] — RICHARD BAXTER

In Heaven, we're told, we will *rest*.
Eden was a picture of rest—with not only sleep and leisure, but also work that was meaningful and enjoyable, abundant food, a beautiful environment, and unhindered friendship with God, other people, and animals. Even with Eden's restful perfection,

one day was set aside for special rest and worship. Work will be refreshing on the New Earth, yet regular rest will be built into our lives.

God rested on the seventh day. He prescribed rest for Adam and Eve before they sinned, and he prescribed it for mankind under sin. Regular rest will be part of the life to come in the new universe. (Wouldn't it be wise to learn how to rest now?)

But will we really have work to do? The idea of working in Heaven is foreign to many. Yet Scripture clearly teaches it.

When God created Adam, he "took the man and put him in the Garden of Eden to work it and take care of it" (Genesis 2:15). Work was part of the original Eden. It was part of a perfect human life on Earth.

Work wasn't part of the Curse, but the Curse made work menial, tedious, and frustrating: "Cursed is the ground because of you; through painful toil you will eat of it all the days of your life. It will produce thorns and thistles for you, and you will eat the plants of the field. By the sweat of your brow you will eat your food" (Genesis 3:17-19).

However, on the New Earth, work will be redeemed and transformed into what God intended: "No longer will there be any curse. The throne of God and of the Lamb will be in the city, and his servants will serve him" (Revelation 22:3). *Serve* is a verb. Servants are people who are active and occupied, carrying out tasks.

God himself is a worker. He didn't create the world and then retire. Jesus said, "My Father is always at his work to this very day, and I, too, am working" (John 5:17). Jesus found great satisfaction in his work. He said, "My food . . . is to do the will of him who sent me and to finish his work" (John 4:34). We'll also have work to do, satisfying and enriching work that will never be drudgery.

In *The Happiness of Heaven*, Father Boudreau argued against Aquinas's belief that Heaven is a place of motionless absorption with an intellectual contemplation of God:

> We are active by nature. Action, therefore, both of mind and body, is a law of our being, which cannot be changed without radically changing, or rather destroying, our whole nature. Instead of destroying it, it follows that in Heaven we shall be far more active than we can possibly be here below.... The soul of Jesus Christ enjoyed the Beatific Vision, even while here on earth in mortal flesh. Was He, on that account, prevented from doing anything except contemplating the divine essence? He certainly was not. He labored and preached; He also drank and slept; He visited His friends and did a thousand other things.[74]

Consider Christ's activities: working in a carpenter shop, walking the countryside, fishing, sailing, meeting people, talking, teaching, eating—doing his life's work. Even after his resurrection he moved from place to place, connecting with his disciples and continuing his work. We might consider this a preview of our coming lives on Earth, after our resurrection.

I'm not just speculating that we'll work on the New Earth; Scripture directly tells us that we will. Upon entering Heaven, what's offered the faithful servant is not retirement but this: "Well done, good and faithful servant; you have been faithful over a few things, I will make you ruler over many things. Enter into the joy of your lord" (Matthew 25:23, NKJV).

Jonathan Edwards said, "The most perfect rest is consistent with being continually employed."

Jesus said to his Father, "I brought glory to you here on earth by completing the work you gave me to do" (John 17:4, NLT).

How will we glorify God for eternity? By doing everything he tells us to do. What did God first tell mankind to do? Fill the earth and exercise dominion over it. What will we do for eternity to glorify God? Exercise dominion over the earth, demonstrate God's creativity and ingenuity as his image-bearers, and produce Christ-exalting culture.

In reflecting on his life's work, writer Victor Hugo spoke profoundly of anticipating his work in Heaven:

> I feel within me that future life. I am like a forest that has been razed; the new shoots are stronger and brighter. I shall most certainly rise toward the heavens. . . . The nearer my approach to the end, the plainer is the sound of immortal symphonies of worlds which invite me. For half a century I have been translating my thoughts into prose and verse: history, philosophy, drama, romance, tradition, satire, ode, and song; all of these I have tried. But I feel I haven't given utterance to the thousandth part of what lies within me. When I go to the grave I can say, as others have said, "My day's work is done." But I cannot say, "My life is done." My work will recommence the next morning. The tomb is not a blind alley; it is a thoroughfare. It closes upon the twilight, but opens upon the dawn.[75]

Not every Christian's *vocation* will continue on the New Earth (morticians, for instance, will be finding new work), but our life's work will continue; our calling to glorify God will never end. That calling will apply as much there and then as it does here and now.

As you work or rest today, will you ask God to help you do it to his glory?

☦ *Lord, on the days when we are so busy and tired and unfinished tasks demand our attention, how wonderful rest sounds to us. After the demands of life, of caring for children and wearing ourselves out at work, what a delight it is to contemplate Heaven as a place of rest. And on the days when we are eager to work, to garden, to study, to design and assemble and build, what a pleasure it is to know that good, productive, enriching work awaits us on the New Earth—work unencumbered by the Curse and done in collaboration with others who will find as much joy in serving Jesus as we will.*

DAY 37

REMEMBERING AND RECOGNIZING

> Brothers, we do not want you to be ignorant about those who fall asleep, or to grieve like the rest of men, who have no hope. . . . [We] will be caught up together with them in the clouds to meet the Lord in the air. And so we will be with the Lord forever. Therefore encourage each other with these words. — 1 Thessalonians 4:13, 17-18

A great multitude of dear ones is there expecting us; a vast and mighty crowd of parents, brothers, and children, secure now of their own safety, anxious yet for our salvation, long that we may come to their right and embrace them, to that joy which will be common to us and to them.[76]
— The Venerable Bede

When we get to Heaven, one writer claims, "We will not even remember this old world we call Earth, . . . nor will we even recall it! It simply will not come into our minds."[77]

This misperception is widely believed, but the Bible says no such thing!

Memory is basic to personality. The principle of redemptive continuity indicates that we will remember our past lives. Heaven cleanses our slate of sin and error, but it doesn't erase our memory of it. The lessons we learned here about God's love, grace, and justice surely aren't lost but will carry over to Heaven. Father Boudreau states, "For the sins which so often made us tremble, are washed away in the blood of Jesus, and are, therefore, no longer a source of trouble. The remembrance of them rather intensifies our love for the God of mercy, and therefore increases our happiness."[78]

Isaiah 65:17 is often cited as proof that in the eternal state we won't remember our present lives: "Behold, I will create new heavens and a new earth. The former things will not be remembered, nor will they come to mind." However, this verse should be viewed in context. It's linked to the previous verse, in which God says, "The past troubles will be forgotten and hidden from my eyes." This doesn't suggest literal lack of memory, as if the omniscient God couldn't recall the past. Rather, it's like God saying, "I will . . . remember their sins no more" (Jeremiah 31:34). It doesn't mean that God has a mental lapse but that he *chooses* not to bring up our past sins or hold them against us. In eternity, former sins and sorrows won't preoccupy God or us. We'll be capable of choosing not to recall or dwell on anything that would diminish Heaven's joy. That is *not* the same as having our memories disappear and our relationships dissolve.

If we forget we were desperate sinners, how could we appreciate the depth and meaning of Christ's redemptive work for us?

We'll never forget that our sins nailed Jesus to the cross; for Christ's resurrection body still has nail-scarred hands and feet (John 20:24-29). Even though God will wipe away the tears and sorrow attached to this world, he will *not* erase human history and Christ's intervention from our minds. As I've said before, Heaven's happiness won't be dependent on our ignorance of what happened on Earth. Rather, it will be enhanced by *perspective*, our informed appreciation of God's glorious grace and justice as we grasp what really happened here.

The Greek word for truth, *aletheia*, is a negated form of the verb "to forget," so that knowing the truth means *to stop forgetting*. On the New Earth, there will be memorials to the twelve tribes and the apostles (Revelation 21:12-14). This indicates continuity and memory of history. If we're aware of other past events on the old Earth, surely we'll be aware of our own.

When asked if we would recognize friends in Heaven, George MacDonald responded, "Shall we be greater fools in Paradise than we are here?"[79]

Yet many people wonder whether we'll know each other in Heaven. It's a question I'm often asked—*but why?* Because of the pervasiveness of Christoplatonism, which teaches that the spiritual is incompatible with the physical. But Christ, in his incarnation and resurrection, laid claim not only to the spiritual realm but to the physical realm as well. His redemption wasn't only of spirits but also of bodies and of the earth. The false assumption behind the question of whether we'll recognize loved ones in Heaven is that we'll be disembodied spirits who lose our identities and memories—and how would someone recognize a spirit?

Christ's disciples recognized him countless times after his resurrection. They recognized him on the shore as he cooked breakfast for them (John 21). They recognized him when he appeared to a skeptical Thomas (John 20:24-29). They recognized him when he appeared to five hundred people at once (1 Corinthians 15:6).

At Christ's transfiguration, his disciples identified Moses and Elijah, even though they couldn't have known what they looked like (Luke 9:29-33). Scripture gives no indication of a memory wipe that would cause us not to recognize family and friends. Paul anticipated being with the Thessalonians in Heaven, and it never occurred to him that he wouldn't know them or recognize them. In fact, if we wouldn't know our loved ones, the "comfort" of an afterlife reunion, taught in 1 Thessalonians 4:14-18, would be no comfort at all.

Missionary Amy Carmichael had strong convictions on this question:

> Shall we know one another in Heaven? Shall we love and remember? I do not think anyone need wonder about this or doubt for a single moment. . . . For if we think for a minute, we know. Would you be yourself if you did not love and remember? . . . We are told that we shall be like our Lord Jesus. Surely this does not mean in holiness only, but in everything; and does not He know and love and remember? He would not be Himself if He did not, and we should not be ourselves if we did not.[80]

Whom do you look forward to seeing again in Heaven? Do you think you'll have a hard time recognizing or remembering them? Do you suppose your memory will be worse, or better? How might God be glorified through our memories?

✠ *Father, thank you that we have every reason to look forward to recognizing and remembering our family and friends in Heaven and rejoicing together in your presence for the lives we shared and the trials we faced together. In that day we will see with clarity your purposes and know without a doubt your goodness and love in the midst of the hard times of loss and confusion and grief we experienced on this earth. Lord, remind us that every good-bye to a loved one who knows you is not the end of our relationship but only an interruption, to be followed by a glorious reunion and grateful remembrance of our shared lives.*

DAY 38

MARRIAGE AND FAMILY

You long to see us, just as we also long to see you. . . . How can we thank God enough for you in return for all the joy we have in the presence of our God because of you? Night and day we pray most earnestly that we may see you again. — 1 Thessalonians 3:6, 9-10

If I knew that never again would I recognize that beloved one with whom I spent more than thirty-nine years here on earth, my anticipation of heaven would much abate. To say that we shall be with Christ and that that will be enough, is to claim that there we shall be without the social instincts and affections which mean so much to us here. . . . Life beyond cannot mean impoverishment, but the enhancement and enrichment of life as we have known it here at its best.[81]
— W. Graham Scroggie

When we receive our glorified bodies and relocate to the New Earth, it will culminate history, not erase it. And nothing will negate or minimize the fact that we were members of families here on Earth. My daughters will always be my daughters, though first and foremost they are God's daughters.

My grandchildren will always be my grandchildren. Heaven won't be without families; it will be *one big happy family*, in which all family members are friends and all friends are family members. We'll have family relationships with people who were our blood relatives on Earth, but we'll also have family relationships with friends, both old and new.

When someone told Jesus that his mother and brothers were wanting to see him, he replied, "My mother and brothers are those who hear God's word and put it into practice" (Luke 8:19-21). Jesus was saying that devotion to God creates a bond that transcends biological family ties.

Jesus also said that those who follow him will gain "brothers, sisters, mothers, children" (Mark 10:29-30). I think of this when I experience an immediate depth of relationship with a fellow Christian I've just met. If you weren't able to have children on Earth or if you've been separated from your children, God will give you relationships, both now and later, that will meet your needs to guide, help, serve, and invest in others. If you've never had a parent you could trust, you'll find trustworthy parents everywhere in Heaven, reminding you of your heavenly Father.

So will there be family in Heaven? Yes, there will be *one* great family—and none of us will ever be left out. Every time we see someone, it will be a family member! (Of course, we can be closer to some family members than to others, but there will be no rivalry or envy or grudges.) Many of us, myself included, treasure our families. But many others have endured a lifetime of broken hearts stemming from twisted family relationships. In Heaven, no one will cause anyone else pain. Our relationships will be rich and harmonious.

But what about marriage?

The Sadducees, who didn't believe in the resurrection of the dead, tried to trick Jesus with a question about marriage in Heaven. Attempting to make him look foolish, they told him of a woman who had seven husbands who all died. They asked him, "Now then, at the resurrection, whose wife will she be of the seven, since all of them were married to her?" (Matthew 22:28).

Christ replied, "At the resurrection people will neither marry nor be given in marriage; they will be like the angels in heaven" (Matthew 22:30).

There's a great deal of misunderstanding about this passage. A woman wrote me, "I struggle with the idea that there won't be marriage in heaven. I believe I'll really miss it."

But the Bible does *not* teach there will be no marriage in Heaven. In fact, it makes it clear there *will* be marriage in Heaven. What it says is that there will be *one* marriage, between Christ and his bride—and we'll all be part of it. Paul links human marriage to the higher reality it mirrors: "'For this reason a man will leave his father and mother and be united to his wife, and the two will become one flesh.' This is a profound mystery—but I am talking about Christ and the church" (Ephesians 5:31-32).

The one-flesh marital union is a signpost pointing to our relationship with Christ as our bridegroom. Once we reach the destination, however, the signpost becomes unnecessary. That one marriage—our marriage to Christ—will be so completely satisfying that even the most wonderful earthly marriage couldn't be as fulfilling. Earthly marriage is a shadow, a copy, an echo, of the true and ultimate marriage. Once that ultimate marriage begins, at the Lamb's wedding feast, all the human marriages that pointed to it will have served their noble purpose and will be assimilated into the one great marriage they foreshadowed. "The purpose of marriage is not to replace Heaven, but to prepare us for it."[82]

The joy of marriage in Heaven will be far greater because of the character and love of our bridegroom. I rejoice for Nanci and for myself that we'll both be married to the most wonderful person in the universe. He's already the one we love most—there is no competition. On Earth, the closer we draw to Christ, the closer we draw to each other. Surely the same will be true in Heaven. What an honor it'll be to know that God chose us for each other on this old Earth so that we might have a foretaste of life with him on the New Earth. I fully expect that Nanci will remain my closest friend besides Jesus himself. And I expect other family relationships not to be lost, but to be deepened and enriched.

Will the deep relationships built in this life vanish in the next life? Or will they more likely start where they left off, and then get better and better? How might God be glorified by relationships with our families that carry over into the next life?

Father, I am profoundly grateful for the wife you've given me. There's no one else on Earth I'd rather be with than her. By growing together in our love for each other, we have grown together in our love for you. We recognize you as our ultimate source of joy. Thank you also for the parents and daughters and sons that you've blessed us with. I look forward to enjoying our relationships together a million years from now. The delight we take in our grandchildren is a gift we cannot put a price on. Thank you, Jesus, that you promise reunion with loved ones who have gone on ahead. Thank you that the best of relationships here will be so much better there, in a world where things will never again take a turn for the worse.

FRIENDSHIPS IN HEAVEN: OLD AND NEW

I tell you, use worldly wealth to gain friends for yourselves, so that when it is gone, you will be welcomed into eternal dwellings. — Luke 16:9

We have not lost our dear ones who have departed from this life, but have merely sent them ahead of us, so we also shall depart and shall come to that life where they will be more than ever dear as they will be better known to us, and where we shall love them without fear of parting.[83] — Augustine

Do you have a close friend who has had a profound influence on you? Do you think it's a coincidence that she was in your dorm wing or became your roommate? Was it accidental that your desk or mailbox was near his, or that her family lived next door, or that your father was transferred when you were in third grade so that you ended up in his neighborhood? God orchestrates our lives. "From one man he made every nation of men, that they should inhabit the whole earth; and he determined the times set for them and the exact places where they should live" (Acts 17:26).

It's no accident which neighborhood you grew up in, who lived next door, who went to school with you, who is part of your church, and who works with you. Our relationships were appointed by God, so there's every reason to believe they'll continue in Heaven. God's plan doesn't stop on the New Earth—it continues. God doesn't abandon his purposes; he extends and fulfills them. God-ordained friendships begun on Earth will continue in Heaven, becoming richer than ever.

When God said, "It is not good for the man to be alone" (Genesis 2:18), he was speaking not only of marriage but also of the general need for human companionship. He was saying, "I'll make these people so that they'll need one another." God delights in his children's love for one another.

Nothing can ever replace the shared experience of loving relationships in the battles and heartaches of life. We are forging a lasting camaraderie like that of soldiers on the battlefield. And when we get to Heaven, we're not likely to forget our common experience of fighting spiritual battles side by side, guarding one another's backs in the trenches of this fallen Earth.

I think of my close friend Steve Keels. We have walked side by side for many years, laughed and cried and prayed together, and been there for each other in times of joy and heartache. Surely such relationships won't diminish in Heaven but will be enhanced.

I envision sitting around a campfire in Heaven, trading stories of the truly exciting times we had on Earth. Times when we turned to our Commander and trusted him to guide and sustain us on long marches. Times when we leaned on our comrades for strength, when we tended to one another and carried and guided one another across the minefields. Times when we basked in the company of family and friends, "fellow citizens with God's people and members of God's household" (Ephesians 2:19).

After speaking of a shrewd servant's desire to use earthly resources so that "people will welcome me into their houses" (Luke 16:4), Jesus told his followers to "use worldly wealth [earthly resources] to gain friends [by making a difference in their lives on Earth]." The reason? "So that when it is gone [when life on Earth is over], you will be welcomed into eternal dwellings" (v. 9).

These friends appear to be those whose lives we've touched on Earth and who now have their own "eternal dwellings." Luke 16:9 seems to say that these "eternal dwellings" are places where we'll stay and fellowship with friends, perhaps as we move about the heavenly Kingdom. Some of these friends may be new ones, but surely many will be people we already know, into whose lives we've already invested.

Do I believe that Jesus is suggesting we'll actually share lodging, meals, and fellowship with friends in God's Kingdom? Yes. I'm aware that some people think this idea is far-fetched. *But why?* Because when we think of Heaven, we don't usually think of resurrected people living on a resurrected Earth, living in dwelling places and eating and sharing together. But that's *exactly* what Scripture teaches us.

Will some friendships be closer than others? Jesus was closer to John than to any of the other disciples. Jesus was closer to Peter, James, and John than to the rest of the Twelve, and closer to the Twelve than to the seventy, and closer to the seventy than to his other followers. He was close to Lazarus and Mary and Martha.

He was so close to his mother that while he was dying on the cross, he instructed John to care for her after his death. If Christ was closer to some people than to others, clearly there can't be anything wrong with that.

In Heaven, there won't be cliques, exclusion, arrogance, posturing, belittling, or jealousy. When friends particularly enjoy each other's company, that's as God designed it. If, as you walk about the New Jerusalem, you see Adam and Eve holding hands as they look at the tree of life, would you begrudge them their special friendship?

Perhaps you're disappointed that you've never had the friendships you long for. In Heaven, you'll have much closer relationships with people you already know, but it's also possible that you haven't yet met the closest friends you'll ever have. Perhaps it will be someone seated next to you at the first great feast. After all, the God who orchestrates friendships will be in charge of the seating arrangements.

On the New Earth, we'll experience the joy of familiarity in old relationships and the joy of discovery in new ones. As we get to know one another better, we'll get to know God better. As we find joy in each other, we'll find joy in him. No human relationships will overshadow our relationship with God. All will serve to enhance it.

The song "Thank You" pictures us in Heaven, meeting people who explain how our giving touched their lives. Every time we give to missions and feed the hungry, we should think about people we'll meet in Heaven. Who knows, some of those very people we're helping and praying for today may one day become our closest friends.

What do you think about the idea of meeting new people and developing new friendships in Heaven? Does the idea excite you?

⇌ *Father, how great to think about friends, both old and new, in Heaven. Thank you that you enjoyed special friendships on Earth. But thank you, too, that your friendships were inclusive. Help us, Lord, to enjoy the friends we have and to look forward to the friendships that await us in your Kingdom, where we will have time and opportunity to rekindle many friendships we've been unable to pursue, maintain those we currently have, and develop new ones. Thank you that you've created us to need other people. Thank you that you meet many of our needs through the friendships you've given us. Help us to anticipate the day when friendships will rise to their highest levels, nourished in your presence.*

DAY 40

LOST OPPORTUNITIES REGAINED

Blessed are you who hunger now, for you will be satisfied.
Blessed are you who weep now, for you will laugh. . . .
Rejoice in that day and leap for joy, because great is your
reward in heaven. — Luke 6:21, 23

He is no fool who gives what he cannot keep to gain what he cannot lose.[84] — Jim Elliot

A young woman visiting a missionary in Eastern Europe asked her, "Isn't it hard being so far away from your [grown] children and missing important events in their lives?"

"Sure," she replied. "But in Heaven we'll have all the time together we want. Right now there's Kingdom work that needs to be done." This woman deeply loves her family and misses them. She treasures time spent with them. But she also knows where her true home is and that life there will be real life. She knows that relationships in God's Kingdom will be even better than the best we've known here.

I believe we'll regain in Heaven whatever we passed up on

Earth in order to faithfully serve God. Doesn't that fit with Christ's promise that those who weep now at their loss will one day laugh in light of their gain?

Consider the millions of Christians who've suffered and died in prison because of their faith, snatched away from their families, deprived of opportunities they craved with children and parents and spouses. Wouldn't it be just like Jesus to reward them on the New Earth with opportunities to do the very things they missed—and far better things as well? Perhaps in some way, on the New Earth, the wives and children of the five missionaries killed in Ecuador in January 1956 by the Auca Indians will receive "comp time" with their loved ones.

Heaven offers more than comfort; it offers *compensation*. In the same way that the hungry will be filled in Heaven and those who weep will laugh, will those who suffer tragedy experience a compensating reward? Maybe my friend Greg, killed as a teenager in a terrible accident, will experience on the New Earth a greater form of the joy he'd have had on this earth had he not died so young. Maybe everything my mother missed because she died when my daughters were young will be hers in Heaven. She was a faithful servant of God and loved her granddaughters. Though I can't prove it, I think God allowed her to watch them get married and become mothers. And one day she'll do more than watch them. I think it's likely that when they're together on the New Earth, they'll enjoy all the time they missed with each other. Maybe those who lost infants to miscarriage and disease and accidents will be given makeup time with them in the new world.

In the movie *Babette's Feast*, a Parisian chef is forced to leave her home through the misfortunes of war. Babette ends up in a windswept Danish coastal village, working as a maid for two women who lead a small, austere Christian sect that frowns on such worldly things as gourmet cooking. Babette grows to love these elderly sisters. When she comes into a large sum of money, she spends it all on giving a single dinner party for the sisters and their friends. It's a picture of God's extravagant grace. Babette realizes that she'll never again be able to afford to give such a gift or to prepare such a meal. One of the sisters is a talented singer who had little opportunity to use her gift. Touched by Babette's generosity, she consoles her: "I feel, Babette, that this is not the end. In Paradise you will be the great artist that God meant you to be! . . . Ah, how you will enchant the angels!"[85]

For those who know God, this sentiment is biblical. He's a God who redeems lost opportunities—especially those lost through our faithful service.

I believe that once the Curse is lifted and death is forever reversed, we may live out many of the "could have beens" taken from us in this life.

One day Nanci read me some letters, translated from Swedish, that were written in 1920 by her grandmother, Ana Swanson, to her family in Sweden. Ana suffered severe health problems. While she was in Montana, being cared for by relatives, her husband, Edwin, was in Oregon, working and caring for their seven children day and night. Ana's letters tell how Edwin wore himself out, got sick, and died. Because Ana was too weak to care for her younger children, they, including Nanci's mother, Adele, were placed for adoption. Ana's letters reflect her broken heart, her nagging guilt . . . *and* her faith in God.

Nanci and I were overcome with tears as we read those letters. What tragic lives. What inconsolable disappointment and pain. Ana and Edwin loved Jesus. They once had great dreams for their lives and family. But poor health, misfortune, separation, and death forever stripped them of each other, their children, and their dreams.

Or did it?

As Nanci and I talked, we considered what God might choose to give this broken family on the New Earth. Perhaps they'll go together to the kind of places they would have gone if health and finances had allowed. Certainly Ana won't be plagued by illness, fatigue, grief, anxiety, and guilt. Isn't it likely that our gracious God, who delights in redemption and renewal and restoration, will give them the wonderful family times they were robbed of on the old Earth?

What did Ana think when she read, "Our present sufferings are not worth comparing with the glory that will be revealed in us" (Romans 8:18)? Perhaps the God of second chances won't merely comfort Ana by removing her grief for what she lost. Perhaps he will in some way actually *restore* what she lost. I believe that God won't just take away suffering; he'll compensate by giving us greater delights than if there had been no suffering. He doesn't merely wipe away tears; he replaces those tears with corresponding joys.

When I visit Ana Swanson on the New Earth, I fully expect to see God's promises fulfilled in her life in the most dramatic, unexpected, and joyful ways.

Have you had some lost opportunities that God might restore on the New Earth? Do you know people you would like to see God reward for their faithfulness by compensating them for what they lost in this life? Do you think it would fit with God's character and the Bible's promises for God to do this?

☨ *Lord, preserve us from the misguided belief that we only go around once on this earth and that this is our only opportunity to enjoy life. Help us to understand that in the world to come you will reward sacrificial decisions and will compensate us for the adversities we faced. Thank you that you did not forget Ana Swanson, who lives with you now. Thank you that you will have her, and millions like her, in mind as you structure our joy-filled home, the New Earth.*

DAY 41

RACES AND NATIONS

The nations will walk by its light, and the kings of the earth will bring their splendor into [the New Jerusalem]. . . . The glory and honor of the nations will be brought into it.   — REVELATION 21:24, 26

As the Lamb of God he will draw all of the goods, artifacts, and instruments of culture to himself; the kings of the earth will return their authority and power to the Lamb who sits upon the throne; Jesus is the one whose blood has purchased a multi-national community, composed of people from every tribe and tongue and nation. His redemptive ministry . . . is cosmic in scope.[86]   — RICHARD MOUW

Will we have ethnic and national identities in Heaven? I believe the biblical answer is yes.

Is the risen Jesus Jewish? Certainly. He will continue to be a descendant of Abraham, Isaac, Jacob, and David. (The fact that he's of the line of David is an essential part of his claim to kingship in Jerusalem.) Will we know Christ is Jewish? Of course. Will our new bodies, which are our old bodies raised to new life and health and vibrancy, still have a genetic code that includes the markers of our ethnic descent? I think so—this continuity is part of what makes our bodies truly *ours*. I see no reason to believe that our resurrection bodies won't have DNA that is intricately designed by God. Our resurrected DNA will be unflawed, but it will preserve our God-designed unique characteristics, racial and otherwise.

Here's what the Bible says: "And they sang a new song with these words: 'You are worthy. . . . Your blood has ransomed people for God from every tribe and language and people and nation. And you have caused them to become a Kingdom of priests for our God. And they will reign on the earth'" (Revelation 5:9-10, NLT). Who will serve as the New Earth's kings and priests? Not people who were *formerly* of every tribe, language, people, and nation, but people who still have these distinctives.

It appears that not only racial but also national distinctions will continue into the eternal Heaven. How do we know this? Because Revelation 21:24-26 unmistakably speaks of nations on the New Earth: "The nations will walk by its light, and the kings of the earth will bring their splendor into [the New Jerusalem]. On no day will its gates ever be shut, for there will be no night there. The glory and honor of the nations will be brought into it." The "splendor" here is likely cultural treasures brought as tribute to Jesus, the King of kings, seated on the throne in Jerusalem.

In Revelation 5:9-10, the word *tribe* refers to a person's clan and family lineage. The word *people* often refers to race, and *nation* refers to those who share a national identity and culture. I believe it is a mistake to view nations and races merely as products of the tower of Babel. As our sovereign Creator, God glorifies himself in our distinctive identities and our unity that transcends them.

Herman Bavinck says of the New Earth, "All those nations—each in accordance with its own distinct national character—bring into the new Jerusalem all they have received from God in the way of glory and honor."[87]

Like the current, earthly Jerusalem, the New Jerusalem will be a melting pot of ethnic diversity. But unlike the current city, the groups in the New Jerusalem will be united by their common worship of King Jesus. They will delight in each other's differences, and never resent or be frightened by them.

Unfortunately, in this world under the Curse, there's often hostility between races and nations. We're divided by sin and intolerant of differences in appearance, language, and culture. Of the racial divide between Jews and Gentiles, Paul says, "For [Christ] himself is our peace, who has made the two one and has destroyed the barrier, the dividing wall of hostility. . . . His purpose was to create in himself one new man out of the two, thus making peace, and in this one body to reconcile both of them to God through the cross, by which he put to death their hostility" (Ephesians 2:14-16).

Christ died for our sins of racism. His work on the cross put racism to death. The redemption of mankind and the earth will include the redemption of human relationships and the uniting of different people groups in Christ. Racist groups that purport to be Christian are the opposite of Christian. There will be no racial prejudice in Heaven. There will be no illusions of ethnic or national superiority, no disputes over borders.

Some scholars argue that the image of God has a corporate

dimension: "There is no one human individual or group who can fully bear or manifest all that is involved in the image of God, so that there is a sense in which that image is collectively possessed. The image of God is, as it were, parceled out among the peoples of the earth. By looking at different individuals and groups, we get glimpses of different aspects of the full image of God."[88]

If this is true, and I believe it may be, then racism is not only an injustice toward people but also a rejection of God's very nature. On the New Earth, we'll never celebrate sin, but we'll celebrate diversity in the biblical sense. We'll never try to keep people out. We'll welcome them in, exercising hospitality to every traveler.

Peace on Earth will be rooted in our common ruler, Christ the King, who alone is the source of "glory to God in the highest, and on earth peace among men with whom He is pleased" (Luke 2:14, NASB). Peace on Earth will not be accomplished by the abolition of our differences but by a unifying loyalty to the King, a loyalty that transcends our differences and is enriched by them. We have so much to learn from each other, and there is so much to be learned about God from the distinct characteristics he has built into the different races and nations.

Are you excited by the idea of racial and national distinctions on the New Earth? How do you think God will be glorified by those distinctions?

Father, thank you that a world awaits us in which the best of every culture and heritage of humanity will be preserved and that everything that dishonors you will be destroyed forever. Thank you that we will forever enjoy the richness of being fellow citizens in your Kingdom, with people of every tribe and nation and language. What a delight it will be to see your character revealed more clearly through different people groups. Help us to dedicate our prayers and our money and our service to the cause of world missions, that we may be your instruments to reach people for Jesus from every tribe, nation, and language. Help us to treat those who are different from us with the deepest respect, including racial minorities and immigrants in our communities, schools, and workplaces. May we be your ambassadors to those who don't know you, and may they find in you what they are looking for deep in their hearts.

THE DEVELOPMENT OF CULTURE

> The Lord God took the man and put him in the Garden of Eden to work it and take care of it.... [Jabal] was the father of those who live in tents and raise livestock. His brother's name was Jubal; he was the father of all who play the harp and flute. Zillah also had a son... who forged all kinds of tools out of bronze and iron.
>
> — Genesis 2:15; 4:20-22

The happiness of heaven is not like the steady, placid state of a mountain lake where barely a ripple disturbs the tranquility of its water. Heaven is more akin to the surging, swelling waves of the Mississippi at flood stage.[89] — Sam Storms

Art, music, literature, crafts, technology, clothing, jewelry, education, food preparation—all are part of society or culture, the creative accomplishments of God's image-bearers. Human creations are an extension of God's own creative works, because he created us to reflect him by being creators.

As humans, we glorify God by taking what he created from nothing and shaping it into things for our own good and for his glory. The entire universe—including angels and living creatures in Heaven—should look at our creative ingenuity, our artistic accomplishments, and see God in us, his image-bearers. If that's true now, how much more will it be true when there's nothing in us to dishonor him?

We should expect the social dynamics from Earth to carry over to the New Earth, except when they're a product of our fallenness or when God reveals otherwise. It's true that with engines have come pollution and fatalities, with printing and publishing have come godless books and magazines, and with television has come the glorification of immorality and materialism. Computers have opened up access to incredibly destructive Internet pornography. The splitting of the atom spawned a destructive bomb and the loss of human life. With medical advances have come abortion and euthanasia. Yet *none of these negative by-products are intrinsic to the cultural advances themselves.* Imagine those advances used purely for righteous purposes, without sin to taint them.

Anthony Hoekema writes, "In the beginning man was given the so-called cultural mandate—the command to rule over the earth and to develop a God-glorifying culture. Because of man's fall into sin, that cultural mandate has never been carried out in the way God intended. Only on the new earth will it be perfectly and sinlessly fulfilled. Only then shall we be able to rule the earth properly."[90]

Would there have been culture without the Fall? Of course. Culture is the inevitable result of mankind using God's gifting, equipping, and calling to rule over creation. After the Fall, Scripture describes developments in farming, the crafting of musical instruments, and metallurgy (Genesis 4:20-22). If God had no interest in those cultural improvements, Scripture wouldn't refer to them. God created his image-bearers to glorify him in creative accomplishments, and he's pleased by them. God is pro-culture; he is the creative artist behind and over human culture.

"The LORD God took the man and put him in the Garden of Eden to work it and take care of it" (Genesis 2:15). In human history, only two people, Adam and Eve, even began to taste what it was like to fulfill God's command to subdue the earth, and they didn't get far. Was God shortsighted? Did he not anticipate this? Has he given up on his original idea? No. He had a plan that would fulfill his original design in greater ways. Resurrected culture will reach ever-expanding heights that no culture has yet seen.

Just as God put Adam and Eve in the Garden of Eden to rule the earth, he will put redeemed mankind in the New Jerusalem to rule the New Earth. Just as he designed Adam and Eve to develop their environment and culture, won't he expect us to use our enhanced skills to develop the New Earth? Rather than start over in an undeveloped garden, God will start us on the New Earth in a well-developed city. But surely he expects us, as his redeemed image-bearers, to develop it further. Indeed, that's how he has made us.

In *The Promise of the Future*, Cornelius Venema writes, "Every legitimate and excellent fruit of human culture will be carried into and contribute to the splendour of life in the new creation. Rather than the new creation being a radically new beginning, in which the excellent and noble fruits of humankind's fulfillment of the cultural mandate are wholly discarded—the new creation will benefit from, and be immensely enriched by, its receiving of these fruits."[91]

Paul Marshall speaks of the prevalent but misguided notion that "we've wrecked the world: what's important now is simply that we rescue people from the wreckage."[92] He calls this *lifeboat theology*: "It is as if the creation were the *Titanic*, and now that we've hit the iceberg of sin, there's nothing left for us to do but get ourselves into lifeboats. The ship is sinking rapidly, God has given up on it and is concerned only with the survival of his people. Any effort we make to salvage God's creation amounts to rearranging the deck chairs. Instead, some say, our sole task is to get into the lifeboats, to keep them afloat, to pluck drowning victims out of the water, and to sail on until we get to heaven where all will be well."[93]

Marshall says this is the assumption and perspective that drives many evangelical Christians. He proposes an alternative to lifeboat theology, which he calls *ark theology*: "Noah's ark saved not only people, but it preserved God's other creatures as well. The ark looked not to flee but to return to the land and begin again. Once the flood subsided, *everyone and everything was intended to return again to restore the earth*" (emphasis added).[94]

God's preservation of mankind, the earth, and animals demonstrates that he hasn't given up on his creation. In fact, he commanded Noah after the Flood to do exactly what he commanded Adam and Eve before the Fall: "Be fruitful and increase in number [and] fill the earth" (Genesis 1:28; 9:1). Noah went out to plant a vineyard (Genesis 9:20), and mankind was back to work again on the earth.

Arthur Roberts writes,
> The rise of human civilization hints at a coming splendor. Civilization has brought health and safety. It has brought

freedom from toil and has provided creative enjoyment to millions of people. How much more will civilization flourish when freed from the curse of sin! Already, we are probing the galaxies. Already, we have catalogued the human genome. When the curse of sin is forever removed, surely human beings in Heaven will become active stewards in completing or extending the universe of things and ideas. The whole creation groans, awaiting human redemption. Civilization is not old; it has barely begun![95]

Does the prospect of renewed and expanded culture on the New Earth excite you? What do you look forward to? How might redeemed human culture glorify God in the ages to come?

Father, thank you that our gifts and passions and special interests are not an accident but are part of the way you have wired us. Thank you that you have intricately designed each one of us to uniquely express your glory. And surely this will be even more true on the New Earth, where we will be forever delivered from everything that hinders us and drags us down. Father, how wonderful it will be to invent, design, and make things to enhance our redeemed culture and to further your glory to the ends of the universe. May our work today be enriched and motivated by this destiny you've set before us.

LAUGHTER

Blessed are you who weep now, for you will laugh.
— Luke 6:21

*And as I knelt beside the brook
To drink eternal life, I took
A glance across the golden grass,
And saw my dog, old Blackie, fast
As she could come. She leaped the stream—
Almost—and what a happy gleam
Was in her eye. I knelt to drink,
And knew that I was on the brink
Of endless joy. And everywhere
I turned I saw a wonder there.*[96] — John Piper

Who said, "If you're not allowed to laugh in heaven, I don't want to go there"? (Hint: It wasn't Mark Twain.)

The answer is, Martin Luther. In Heaven, I believe our joy will often erupt in laughter. When laughter is prompted by what's appropriate, God always takes pleasure in it. I think Christ will laugh with us, and his wit and fun-loving nature will be our greatest sources of endless laughter.

Where did humor originate? Not with people, angels, or Satan. God created all good things, including good humor. If God didn't have a sense of humor, human beings, as his image-bearers, wouldn't either. Of course, if God didn't have a sense of humor, we probably also wouldn't have aardvarks, baboons, platypuses, and giraffes. You have to smile when you picture one of these, don't you?

There's nothing like the laughter of dear friends. The Bible often portrays us around the dinner table in God's coming Kingdom. What sound do you hear when friends gather to eat and talk? The sound of laughter.

My wife, Nanci, loves football. She opens our home to family and friends for Monday night football. Right now there are five toddlers in the group, and they keep us laughing. If you came to our house on Monday nights, you'd hear cheers and groans for the football teams, but the dominant sound in the room, week after week, is laughter. There are stories from family and work, and heart-to-heart talks, and pausing to pray—all surrounded by laughter. God made us to laugh and to love to laugh.

The new universe will ring with laughter. Am I just speculating about this? No. I can point to Scripture worth memorizing. Jesus said, "Blessed are you who hunger now, for you will be satisfied. Blessed are you who weep now, for you will laugh" (Luke 6:21). *You will laugh.*

Where will we be satisfied? In Heaven. Where will we laugh? In Heaven. Can we be certain of that? Yes, because Jesus tells us precisely where this promise will be fulfilled: "Rejoice in that day and leap for joy, because great is your reward in heaven" (Luke 6:23).

Just as Jesus promises satisfaction as a reward in Heaven, he also promises laughter as a reward. Anticipating the laughter to come, Jesus says we should "leap for joy" now. Can you imagine someone leaping for joy in utter silence, without laughter? Take any group of rejoicing people, and what do you hear? Laughter. There may be hugging, backslapping, playful wrestling, singing, and storytelling. *But always there is laughter.* It is God's gift to humanity. Surely laughter will not contract, but expand in the final resurrection.

The reward of those who mourn now will be laughter later. Passages such as Luke 6 gave the early Christians strength to endure persecution in "an understanding of heaven as the compensation for lost earthly privileges."[97] In early Christian Greek tradition, Easter Monday was a "day of joy and laughter," called Bright Monday. Only the followers of Christ can laugh in the face of persecution and death because they know that their present trouble isn't all there is. They know that someday they will laugh.

By God's grace, we can laugh right now, even under death's shadow. Jesus doesn't say, "If you weep, soon things on Earth will take a better turn, and then you'll laugh." Things won't always take a better turn on an Earth under the Curse. Sickness, loss, grief, and death will find us. Just as our reward will come in Heaven, laughter (itself one of our rewards) will come in Heaven, compensating for our present sorrow. God won't only wipe away all our tears, he'll fill our hearts with joy and our mouths with laughter.

Those who are poor, diseased, and grieving experience therapeutic laughter. At memorial services, people laugh quickly. The best carefree moments on Earth bring laughter. And if we can laugh hard now—in a world full of poverty, disease, and disasters—then surely what awaits us in Heaven is far greater laughter.

One of Satan's great lies is that God—and goodness—is joyless and humorless, while Satan—and evil—bring pleasure and satisfaction. In fact, it's Satan who's humorless. Sin didn't bring him joy; it forever stripped him of joy. In contrast, envision Jesus with his disciples. If you cannot picture Jesus teasing them and laughing with them, you need to reevaluate your theology of Creation and Incarnation. We need a biblical theology of humor that prepares us for an eternity of celebration, spontaneous laughter, and overflowing joy.

C. S. Lewis depicts laughter in Heaven when his characters attend the Great Reunion on the New Narnia: "And there was greeting and kissing and handshaking and old jokes revived (you've no idea how good an old joke sounds after you take it out again after a rest of five or six hundred years)."[98]

Who's the most intelligent, creative, witty, and joyful human being in the universe? Jesus Christ. Whose laughter will be loudest and most contagious on the New Earth? Jesus Christ's.

When you face difficulty and discouragement, keep your eyes on joy's source. Recite Christ's promise for the new world, a promise that echoes off the far reaches of the universe: *You will laugh.*

Do you look forward to laughter in Heaven? Are you experiencing the joy of Christ so that there is plenty of laughter in your life now?

⇌ Father, today, right now, feeling as we do, with deadlines and health issues and friends who are hurting and world events in flux, we need to hear your promise that in

Heaven we will laugh. We picture Jesus, laughing with his disciples, and we can't wait to hear his laugh in person. We look forward to laughing with him at banquets and on walks and in conversations. Thank you for the gift of laughter. Thank you that you invented it. Thank you that we do not have to wait until Heaven to laugh, but that laughter can carry us on its back through difficult times. We think of the release that laughter brings at memorial services for people who have followed you faithfully, people who are already laughing on death's other side. We have enjoyed rich laughter, mingled with tears, with friends and family in difficult days. When we weep now, Father, remind us that in Heaven, partaking of your joy, we will laugh.

DAY 44

NO MORE BOREDOM

In Your presence is fullness of joy; at Your right hand are pleasures forevermore. — Psalm 16:11, NKJV

Imaginary evil is romantic and varied; real evil is gloomy, monotonous, barren, boring. Imaginary good is boring; real good is always new, marvelous, intoxicating.

— Simone Weil

Science fiction writer Isaac Asimov said, "I don't believe in an afterlife, so I don't have to spend my whole life fearing hell, or fearing heaven even more. For whatever the tortures of hell, I think the boredom of heaven would be even worse."

Sadly, even among Christians, it's a prevalent myth that Heaven will be boring. Sometimes we can't envision anything beyond strumming a harp and polishing streets of gold. We've succumbed to Satan's strategies "to blaspheme God, and to slander his name and his dwelling place" (Revelation 13:6).

People sometimes say, "I'd rather be having a good time in Hell than be bored out of my mind in Heaven." Many imagine Hell as a place where they'll hang around and shoot pool and joke with friends. That could happen on the New Earth, but not in Hell.

Hell is a place of torment and isolation, where friendship and good times don't exist. Hell will be deathly boring. Everything good, enjoyable, refreshing, fascinating, and interesting originates with God. Without God, there's nothing interesting to do. David wrote, "In Your presence is fullness of joy; at Your right hand are pleasures forevermore" (Psalm 16:11, NKJV). Conversely, outside of God's presence, there is no joy.

Our belief that Heaven will be boring betrays a heresy—that *God* is boring. There's no greater nonsense. What's true is that our desire for pleasure and the experience of joy come directly from God's hand. God designed and gave us our taste buds, adrenaline, sex drives, and the nerve endings that convey pleasure to our brains. Likewise, our imaginations and our capacity for joy and exhilaration were *made by the very God we accuse of being boring*! Do we imagine that we ourselves came up with the idea of fun?

"Won't it be boring to be good all the time?" Note the underlying assumption: Sin is exciting, righteousness is boring. We've fallen for the devil's lie. His most basic strategy, the same one he employed with Adam and Eve, is to make us believe that sin brings fulfillment. But the opposite is true. Sin robs us of fulfillment. Sin doesn't make life interesting; it makes life empty. Sin doesn't create adventure; it blunts it. Sin doesn't expand life; it shrinks it. Sin's emptiness inevitably leads to boredom. When there's fulfillment, when there's beauty, when we see God as he truly is—an endless reservoir of fascination—boredom becomes impossible.

Those who believe there can't be excitement without sin think with sin-poisoned minds. Drug addicts are convinced that without their drugs they can't live happy lives. In fact—as everyone else can see—drugs make them miserable. Freedom from sin will mean freedom to be what God intended, freedom to find far greater joy in everything. In Heaven we'll be filled, as Psalm 16:11 describes it, with joy and eternal pleasures.

Another reason why people assume Heaven is boring is that their Christian lives are boring. That's not God's fault. He calls us to follow him in an adventure that should put us on life's edge. If we're experiencing the invigorating stirrings of God's Spirit, trusting him to fill our lives with divine appointments, and experiencing the childlike delights of his gracious daily kindnesses, then we'll know that God is exciting and Heaven is exhilarating. What else *could* they be?

As for having nothing to do in Heaven, we're going to help God run the universe (Luke 19:11-27). We'll have an eternity full of things to do. The Bible's picture of resurrected people at work in a vibrant society on a resurrected earth couldn't be more compelling. (No wonder Satan works so hard to rob us of it.)

God will give us renewed minds and marvelously constructed bodies, full of energy and vision. James Campbell says, "The work on the other side, whatever be its character, will be adapted to each one's special aptitude and powers. It will be the work he can do best; the work that will give the fullest play to all that is within him."[99]

Even under the Curse, we catch glimpses of how work can be enriching, how it can build relationships, and how it can help us to improve ourselves and our world. Work stretches us in ways that make us smarter, wiser, and more fulfilled.

The God who created us to do good works (Ephesians 2:10)

will not abandon this purpose when he resurrects us to inhabit the new universe.

We are told that we will serve God in Heaven (Revelation 7:15; 22:3). Service is active, not passive. It involves fulfilling responsibilities, in which we expend energy. Work in Heaven won't be frustrating or fruitless; it will involve lasting accomplishments, unhindered by decay and fatigue, and enhanced by unlimited resources. We'll approach our work in Heaven with the same enthusiasm we now bring to our favorite sports or hobbies.

In Heaven, we'll reign with Christ, exercise leadership and authority, and make important decisions. This implies specific delegated responsibilities for those under our leadership, as well as specific responsibilities given to us by our leaders (Luke 19:17-19). We'll set goals, devise plans, and share ideas. Our best workday on Earth—when everything turns out better than we planned, when we get everything done on time, when everyone on the team pulls together and enjoys each other—is just a small foretaste of the joy our work will bring us on the New Earth.

If you think that life in God's new universe will be boring, *you're just not getting it.* Imagine the flowers that botanists will study (and enjoy), the animals that zoologists will research (and play with). Gifted astronomers may go from star system to star system, galaxy to galaxy, studying the wonders of God's creation. A disembodied existence would be boring, but our resurrection to bodily life on the New Earth will forever put boredom to death.

Of all the exciting things we may do in Heaven for God's glory, what are some you most look forward to?

⇌ *Father, forgive us for the times we have embraced Satan's favorite heresy that Heaven will be boring, that you are dull, and that your people in Heaven will wish we were elsewhere. Rescue us from our wrong views of Heaven. Rescue us especially from the twisted notion that sin is more interesting than righteousness, and from the heresy that disobeying you will bring excitement rather than destruction. Help us to realize that the world will try to sell these lies to our children and that it is our job to take them to your Word and show them the truth about Heaven that's so captivating and exciting. God, help us today to model Heaven's joy to our families, friends, neighbors, and coworkers.*

DAY 45

DREAMS FULFILLED

Blessed are you who are poor, for yours is the kingdom of God. Blessed are you who hunger now, for you will be satisfied. Blessed are you who weep now, for you will laugh. Blessed are you when men hate you, when they exclude you and insult you and reject your name as evil, because of the Son of Man. Rejoice in that day and leap for joy, because great is your reward in heaven.
— Luke 6:20-23

For three things I thank God every day of my life: thanks that he has vouchsafed me knowledge of his works; deep thanks that he has set in my darkness the lamp of faith; deep, deepest thanks that I have another life to look forward to—a life joyous with light and flowers and heavenly song.
— Helen Keller

Many people believe that this life is all there is. Their philosophy? "You only go around once, so grab what you can."

But if you're a child of God, you do *not* just "go around once" on Earth. You don't get just one earthly life. You'll get another one, far better and without end. You'll inhabit the New Earth. As an undying person on an undying Earth, you'll live with the God you cherish and the people you love—forever. Those who go to Hell are the ones who only go around once on this earth.

Think of all the unfulfilled dreams throughout human history. You've probably experienced some yourself, haven't you? Looking back, do you wish you'd been able to go certain places and do certain things? Perhaps it was your commitment to help others that kept you from living out those dreams. Some people are embittered by this. Others are simply sad. Life seems to have broken its promises, and some people end up regretting years of unfulfilled dreams.

But God is not unjust, and he is not uncaring. And this is *not* our only chance at life on Earth. Luke 6:20-24 promises blessings in Heaven for the difficulties we face now. We're told that when we face affliction for following Christ, we're to "rejoice in that day and leap for joy, because great is [our] reward in heaven" (Luke 6:24).

Where will this Heaven be? On Earth. In Matthew 5:3-5, Jesus says, "Blessed are the poor in spirit, for theirs is the kingdom of heaven. Blessed are those who mourn, for they will be comforted. Blessed are the meek, for they will inherit the earth." *Earth* is the setting for God's ultimate comfort, for his reversal of life's injustices and tragedies. All the blessings of Heaven that Jesus promised us will be ours in the place where we'll live forever—the New Earth.

That's why I believe that the New Earth will be a place where missed opportunities will be regained. That's also one reason why I believe that on the New Earth people who lost their spouses or children may be able to experience much of what they missed on the old Earth, and a great deal more. God promises not only to remove the heartbreaks of this earth but to make up for them. We will feast instead of going hungry; we'll be rich instead of being poor, at peace rather than being persecuted. The New Earth will be a place where we will experience the fulfillment of deep longings and God-given dreams that died or were crushed in this life.

Are you living with the disappointment of unfulfilled dreams? In Heaven, you'll find their fulfillment! Did poverty, poor health, war, or lack of time prevent you from pursuing an adventure or a dream? Did you never get to finish building that boat or painting that picture or writing that book—or reading that pile of books? Good news. The New Earth will be a second chance to do what you dreamed of, and far more besides.

In my novel *Safely Home*, I tell the story of Li Quan, a brilliant Chinese man whose dream was to write and teach in a university. Persecution for his faith in Christ robbed him of that opportunity. He worked instead as an assistant locksmith, in faithfulness and humility. He never saw his dreams fulfilled on Earth, but later in Heaven, as I imagined it, Christ gives Li Quan an assignment—to write and teach.

We don't want to live as some sort of disembodied creatures in an alien world. We want to be sinless, healthy people living on Earth, but without the fighting, disease, disappointment, and death. We want to be the kind of people and live in the kind of world where our dreams, the deepest longings of our hearts, really do come true. That is exactly what God's Word promises us.

We are hurt in countless ways when we fail to grasp this. We become discouraged, supposing that we'll never know the joy of what we desire. People who are disabled may fear that they'll never run in a meadow or know the pleasure of swimming. People who have never married—or who don't have a good marriage—may fear that they'll never know the joy that marriage can bring.

On the New Earth, in perfect bodies, we'll run through meadows and swim in pristine waters. We'll have the most exciting and fulfilling marriage there's ever been, a marriage so glorious and complete that there will be no reason for another. Jesus himself will be our bridegroom.

The smartest person God ever created in this world may never have learned to read because he or she had no opportunity. The most musically gifted person may never have touched a musical instrument. The greatest athlete may never have competed in a game. The sport you're best at may be a sport you've never tried, your favorite hobby one you've never thought of. Living under the Curse means we've missed many opportunities. But when the Curse is reversed, at the resurrection, we'll regain opportunities and inherit many more besides.

Without an eternal perspective, without understanding the reality that the best is yet to come, we assume that people who die young, are handicapped, aren't healthy, don't get married, or don't _____ [fill in the blank] will inevitably miss out on the best life has to offer. But the theology underlying those assumptions is fatally flawed. We're presuming that our present Earth, bodies, cultures, relationships, and lives are superior to those of the New Earth.

What are we thinking?

Are there some dreams you have had that you think might be from God, but you've not seen them fulfilled? If they are not fulfilled in this life, do you think they may be, in some form, in the next life?

☩ *Father, preserve us from the illusion that this life, in these bodies, on the earth as it now is, constitutes the limits of our life opportunities. Help us to understand what it will mean to have new bodies and to live on the New Earth, where problems of insufficient health and wealth and time will never limit what we can do and where we can go and what we can see. Take off our blinders, Lord, and open our eyes to the world of new and greater opportunities that await us in Heaven. Thank you that our greatest dreams will one day be fulfilled on the New Earth.*

DAY 46

NEW OPPORTUNITIES ON THE NEW EARTH

Whoever can be trusted with very little can also be trusted with much. — Luke 16:10

I haven't been cheated out of being a complete person—I'm just going through a forty-year delay, and God is with me even through that. Being "glorified"—I know the meaning of that now. It's the time, after my death here, when I'll be on my feet dancing.[100] — Joni Eareckson Tada

The subject of unfulfilled dreams and missed opportunities, as it relates to Heaven, is rarely discussed. But I think it's worthy of further consideration. My heart resonates with the words of Robert Browning:

Grow old along with me!
The best is yet to be,
The last of life, for which the first was made.[101]

Unfortunately, most older couples reach a time when those blissful words ring hollow. Disease, senility, incapacity, or accidents inevitably come and eventually bring death, and with it separation from one's beloved spouse, a heartbreaking ending. Then Browning's lovely words may haunt us. Old age and the "last of life," romanticized in the poem, can be brutal, devastating, sad, and lonely.

Nanci and I both saw our dear mothers die, then watched helplessly as our fathers got old and frail in body and mind. From a human perspective, we felt hopeless because they'd been at their physical and mental peaks many years earlier, yet all they could do now was slide downhill.

But a biblical perspective corrected our natural misperceptions. Scripture informed us that God has a purpose for every person who's still here—and that after a brief period of deterioration, our parents would go to Heaven and immediately be relieved of their hardships. Then, one day God will raise them, and they'll have new minds and bodies, ready to start over again on a New Earth.

Consider cosmetic surgeries, implants, and other attempts at remodeling and renovating our crumbling bodies. We hold on to youthfulness with a white-knuckled grip. Ultimately it's all in vain. But the gospel promises us eternal youthfulness, health, and beauty. It's not ours now—but it will be, at the resurrection, which will be the true fountain of youth.

Peter Toon expresses the disappointment we often feel, and the hope we can have:

> The most tragic strain in human existence lies in the fact that the pleasure which we find in the things of this life, however good that pleasure may be in itself, is always

taken away from us. The things for which men strive hardly ever turn out to be as satisfying as they expected, and in the rare cases in which they do, sooner or later they are snatched away.... For the Christian, all those partial, broken and fleeting perfections which he glimpses in the world around him, which wither in his grasp and are snatched away from him even while they wither, are found again, perfect, complete and lasting in the absolute beauty of God.[102]

Do you believe that God is big enough to fulfill your dreams?

When you experience disappointment and loss as you faithfully serve God, remember that the loss is temporary but the gains will be eternal. Every day on the New Earth will be a new opportunity to live out the dreams that matter most.

When we're young, we dream of becoming astronauts, professional athletes, or great musicians. As we get older, our dreams shrink, and "realism" sinks in: We'll never be able to fulfill most of our dreams. The death of idealism robs us of our youthfulness and vitality. We become cynical and lose the sense of awe and wonder our dreams once infused us with.

But when we realize that God calls us to be like children and that he'll give us a new universe and unlimited time, then we suddenly "get it." We realize we'll yet have an opportunity to fulfill our dreams. In fact, we'll develop bigger dreams than we ever had, and fulfill those, too. Our dreams will expand, not shrink.

When the Curse is reversed, shrunken dreams will be revived and enhanced. Perhaps that's part of what it means to become like a little child and why childlikeness is necessary for Heaven.

Children aren't disillusioned, hopeless, and cynical. Their dreams are great and broad. They don't list a hundred reasons why their dreams can't come true. Their dreams fuel their imaginations and bring them joy.

At the end of Peter Jackson's production of Tolkien's *Return of the King*, Bilbo Baggins—extremely old and decrepit—is invited to board an Elven ship to sail from Middle Earth to Valinar (a sort of intermediate Heaven). He smiles, and a youthful energy returns to his eyes as he says, "I think I'm quite ready for another adventure."

For the Christian, death is not the end of adventure, but a doorway from a world where dreams and adventures shrink to a world where dreams and adventures forever expand.

As we head toward our future on the New Earth, we'll lose time and countless opportunities here—but we'll regain them there. And the better we use our time and opportunity for God's glory now, the greater will be our opportunities there (Luke 16:11-12; 19:17).

For believers, words more accurate than Robert Browning's would be these: "The best is yet to be, the *next* of lives, for which the *first* was made."

The last of our lives before we die is in fact not the last of our lives! We'll go right on living in another place. And one day, after our bodily resurrection, we'll live again on Earth, a life so rich and joyful that this life will seem impoverished in comparison.

Millions of years from now we'll still be young.

Do you feel ready for the great adventure—the greatest adventure of your life—that awaits you on the other side of death?

☩ *Lord, help us to see the world ahead as a great adventure. Help us to realize that the best is yet to be—the next of lives, for which this first was made. Help us to loosen our white-knuckled grip on appearing young and embrace the promise of eternal youth through our bodily resurrection. Help us to trade in our worn-out dreams and accept in exchange the eternal dreams of the risen Christ. Your dreams for us, Lord, revealed in your Word, are so much greater than the little dreams we so often settle for. May we never be content with less than you offer and promise—and what you died to grant us.*

PLUS ULTRA: MORE BEYOND

The path of the righteous is like the light of dawn, that shines brighter and brighter until the full day.
— PROVERBS 4:18, NASB

What is the essence of heaven? . . . [It is the] beatific vision, love, and enjoyment of the triune God. For the three divine persons have an infinitely perfect vision and love and enjoyment of the divine essence and of one another. And in this infinite knowing, loving and enjoying lies the very life of the triune God, the very essence of their endless and infinite happiness. If the blessed are to be endlessly and supremely happy, then, they must share in the very life of the triune God, in the divine life that makes them endlessly and infinitely happy.[103]
— E. J. FORTMAN

After Columbus discovered the new world, Spain minted coins with the Latin slogan *Plus Ultra*. It meant "More Beyond." This was a horizon-expanding message to people who'd always believed that the world they knew was all there was.

Plus Ultra—there will always be more to discover about our God. In his new universe, there will *always* be more beyond.

I had the privilege of spending two hours alone with Campus Crusade founder Bill Bright six months before he died. As he sat with tubes running to his oxygen tank, he almost jumped out of his chair as we talked about Heaven and the God he loved. This wasn't a man past his peak; he was leaning toward it. "But the path of the righteous is like the light of dawn, that shines brighter and brighter until the full day" (Proverbs 4:18, NASB). This was true of Bill Bright. Though he was nearing death, his eyes and smile looked younger. This was a man who knew there was "more beyond." And now he knows it more than ever. One day all followers of Jesus will know it. But the good news is that we don't have to wait to die to figure that out! (Bill Bright knew it before he died—and we should know it too.)

Five minutes after we die, we'll know exactly how we should have lived. We'll know how we should have given, prayed, shared our faith, meditated on Scripture. But then it will be too late to go back and live our lives over again. We won't have a chance to become sold-out disciples of Jesus Christ in a fallen world. Here and now is our only opportunity to do that.

Ask yourself, "Five minutes after I die, what will I wish I would have done in this life while I still had the chance?" When you come up with the answer, *why not do it now?* Why not spend the rest of your life closing the gap between what you'll wish you would have done and what you actually did?

If dying and going to be with Christ is really "better by far," as Paul tells us in Philippians 1:23, why are so many Christians today afraid to die? I think the answer is that we have stored up our treasures here on Earth—and we don't want to be separated from our treasures.

Jesus commanded us, "Store up for yourselves treasures in heaven" (Matthew 6:20). His logic was that treasures on Earth won't last, and treasures in Heaven will. Hence, storing up treasures on Earth isn't just wrong, it's foolish. And storing up treasures in Heaven isn't just right, it's smart.

Tragically, many Christians store up most of their treasures on Earth. So every day that moves them closer to death moves them farther from their treasures. They end up backing into eternity, *heading away from their treasures*, clinging to a fallen world that hasn't been especially kind to them.

Christ calls us to *turn it around*—to store up our treasures in Heaven. That way, every day we get closer to our deaths, we move *toward* our treasures.

People who spend their lives moving away from their treasures have reason to despair. People who spend their lives moving toward their treasures have reason to rejoice. Are you moving away from your treasures or moving toward them? Are you despairing or rejoicing?

At 2:30 a.m., on November 19, 2002, I stood on our deck gazing up at the night sky. Above me was the Leonid meteor shower, the finest display of celestial fireworks until the year 2096. For someone who has enjoyed meteor showers since he was a kid, this was the celestial event of a lifetime.

There was only one problem: clouds covered the Oregon sky. Of the hundreds of streaking meteors above me, I couldn't see a single one. I felt like a blind man being told, "You're missing the most beautiful sunset of your lifetime. You'll never be able to see another like it."

Was I disappointed? Sure. After searching in vain for small cracks in the cloud cover, I went inside and wrote these paragraphs. I'm disappointed, but not disillusioned. Why? Because I did *not* miss the celestial event of my lifetime.

My lifetime is forever. My residence will be a new universe, with far more spectacular celestial wonders, and I'll have the ability to look through the clouds or rise above them.

During a spectacular meteor shower a few years earlier, I had stood on our deck watching a clear sky. Part of the fun was hearing oohs and aahs in the distance, from neighbors looking upward. Multiply these oohs and aahs by ten thousand times ten thousand, and it'll suggest our thunderous response to what our Father will do in the new heavens as we look upward from the New Earth.

Just as we are not past our prime, the earth and planets and stars and galaxies are not past their prime. They're a dying phoenix that will rise again into something far greater—something that will never die.

I can't wait to see the really great meteor showers and the truly spectacular comets and star systems and galaxies of the new universe. And I can't wait to stand gazing at them alongside once-blind friends who lived their lives on Earth always hearing about what they were missing. Some believed they would never be able to see, regretting the images and events of a lifetime beyond their ability to perceive. The hidden beauties *will* be revealed to them, and to us.

Plus Ultra. There is more beyond. *Much* more. Those of us who know Jesus will be there to behold an endless revelation of natural wonders—likely including spectacular meteor showers that display God's glory—with nothing to block our view.

Are you investing in the world beyond, which promises so much more than the present world? Are you making choices today to put your treasures in Heaven, not on Earth?

⇌ Lord God, help us, with the time and gifts and money you have entrusted to us, to lay up our treasures in Heaven, so that every day we are moving toward our treasures, not away from them. May those things that will be most important to us five minutes after we die become most important to us now.

DAY 48

NO RIVALRY BETWEEN CHRIST AND HEAVEN

They were longing for a better country—a heavenly one.
Therefore God is not ashamed to be called their God,
for he has prepared a city for them. — Hebrews 11:16

*Thy presence makes our Paradise, and where Thou art
is Heaven.*[104] — John Milton

Is it wrong for Christians to daydream about what Scripture tells us awaits us on the other side of death's door? Is it wrong to anticipate entering into a world without suffering and pain, and having a body and mind that work again, and being with loved ones from whom we've been separated? In other words, is it really a good thing to think about Heaven?

Any bride in love with her husband wants to be with him more than anything. But if he goes away for a time to build a beautiful place for her, won't she get excited about it? Won't she think about it and talk about it? Of course she will. Moreover, her husband *wants* her to! If he tells her, "I'm going to prepare a place for you," he's implying, "I want you to look forward to it." Her love and longing for the place he's preparing—where she will live with her husband—is inseparable from her love and longing for him.

Some people erroneously assume that the wonders, beauties, adventures, and marvelous relationships of Heaven must somehow be in competition with God, the one who created them. But God has no fear that we'll get too excited about Heaven. After all, the wonders of Heaven aren't *our* idea, they're *his*. There's no dichotomy between anticipating the joys of Heaven and finding our joy in Christ. It's all part of the same package. The wonders of the new heavens and New Earth will be a primary means by which God reveals himself and his love to us.

Picture Adam and Eve in the Garden of Eden. Eve says to Adam, "Isn't this place magnificent? The sun feels wonderful on my face, the blue sky is gorgeous, and these animals are a delight. Try the mango—it's delicious!"

Imagine Adam responding, "Your focus is all wrong, Eve. You shouldn't think about beauty, refreshment, and mouthwatering fruit. All you should think about is God."

Adam would never say that, because in thinking about these things, Eve *would be* thinking about God. Likewise, our enjoyment of what God has provided us should be inseparable from worshiping, glorifying, and appreciating him. God is honored by our thankfulness, gratitude, and enjoyment of him.

Thinking about Heaven shouldn't be viewed as an *obstacle* to knowing God but as a *means* of knowing him. The infinite God reveals himself to us in tangible, finite expressions. Next to the incarnate Christ, Heaven will tell us more about God than anything else. Some people have told me, "I just want to be with

Jesus—I don't care if Heaven's a shack." Well, Jesus cares, and the place he's preparing for us is no shack. He *wants* us to anticipate Heaven and to enjoy the magnificence of it.

Every thought of Heaven should move our hearts toward God, just as every thought of God will move our hearts toward Heaven. Paul could tell us to set our hearts on Heaven, not just "set your hearts on God," because to do one is to do the other. Heaven will not be an idol that competes with God; it will be a lens by which we see God more clearly.

If we think unworthy thoughts about Heaven, we think unworthy thoughts about God. That's why the conventional caricatures of Heaven do a terrible disservice to God and adversely affect our relationship with him. If we come to love Heaven more—the Heaven that God portrays in Scripture—we will inevitably love God more. If Heaven fills our hearts and minds, God will fill our hearts and minds.

Realizing all this can help us appreciate the sentiments behind a depiction of the believer's death that I sometimes read at memorial services:

> I'm standing on the seashore. A ship at my side spreads her white sails to the morning breeze and starts for the blue ocean. She's an object of beauty and strength and I stand and watch her until, at length, she hangs like a speck of white cloud just where the sea and the sky come down to mingle with each other. And then I hear someone at my side saying, "There, she's gone."
>
> Gone where? Gone from my sight, that is all. She is just as large in mast and hull and spar as she was when

she left my side. And just as able to bear her load of living freight to the place of destination. Her diminished size is in *me*, not in her.

And just at the moment when someone at my side says, "There, she's gone," there are other eyes watching her coming, and there are other voices ready to take up the glad shout, "Here she comes!" And that is dying.[105]

Do you think Jesus wants you to long for Heaven and look forward to being there with him? Why not thank him now for the price he paid to secure your place in Heaven?

⨯ Lord, help us to want more than anything to be with you. As a bride longs to live with her groom, help us desire to live with you. Help us not to feel guilty for looking forward to living in the place that Jesus promised he would prepare for us. As your people have always longed for a better country, a heavenly one, help us to long for what awaits us on the other side of death. For those facing death and for those whose loved ones may be about to die, I pray that you would give them grace and mercy. Help us to believe and be comforted by the truth that just as those here will be saying, "She's gone," those in a better world will be saying, "Here she comes!"

DAY 49

REEPICHEEP AND EMILY

My Father will love him, and we will come to him and make our home with him. — John 14:23

It ought to be the business of every day to prepare for our last day. — Matthew Henry

In C. S. Lewis's *The Voyage of the "Dawn Treader,"* a ship sails east in search of lost countrymen and new adventures. One passenger, Reepicheep, the valiant mouse, is an optimist in the biblical sense. His heart is steadfastly set on a greater adventure. He has one destination in mind: Aslan's country. Heaven.

Reepicheep, standing two feet tall on the *Dawn Treader*'s deck, searches the horizon for Aslan the Lion and for Aslan's country. King Aslan has come to Narnia from the east before, so it's eastward they sail, and eastward Reepicheep gazes with longing.

From his youth, Reepicheep was taught in a poem that one day he would journey to the far east and find what he'd always longed for:

Where sky and water meet,
Where the waves grow sweet,

Doubt not, Reepicheep,
To find all you seek,
There is the utter east.

After reciting the poem to his shipmates, Reepicheep says, "I do not know what it means. But the spell of it has been on me all my life!"[106]

Late in the journey, when they have sailed farther than anyone on record, Reepicheep is thrown into the sea. To his surprise, the water tastes sweet. His excitement is unrestrainable. He's so close to Aslan's country, he can literally taste it.

Reepicheep and the three children go on alone, in a small boat. Then, when the water becomes too shallow, Reepicheep disembarks on his own tiny boat, leaving behind the world he'd always known, with eyes only for his King and his King's country.

Earlier in the voyage, Reepicheep expressed his utter abandonment to seeking Aslan's country: "While I can, I sail east in the *Dawn Treader*. When she fails me, I paddle east in my coracle. When she sinks, I shall swim east with my four paws. And when I can swim no longer, if I have not reached Aslan's country, or shot over the edge of the world in some vast cataract, I shall sink with my nose to the sunrise."[107]

This is Reepicheep's glorious quest. We understand, because the spell of Heaven has been on our lives, too, even if we have sometimes misinterpreted it as lesser desires. At the book's end, the children watch as Reepicheep disappears over the horizon. Does he make it to Aslan's country? In the final book of the Chronicles of Narnia we discover the answer. (Even if you haven't read the book, I'll bet you can guess.)

Let me tell you another story, one that really happened. When five-year-old Emily Kimball was hospitalized and heard she was going to die, she started to cry. Even though she loved Jesus and wanted to be with him, she didn't want to leave her family behind. Then her mother had an inspired idea. She asked Emily to step through a doorway into another room, and she closed the door behind her. One at a time, the entire family started coming through the door to join her. Her mother explained that this was how it would be. Emily would be the first to go through death's door into Heaven. Eventually, the rest of the family would follow, probably one by one, joining her on the other side. Emily understood.

The analogy would have been even more complete if someone representing Jesus had been in the room to greet her—along with departed loved ones and Bible characters and angels.

Every person reading this book is dying. Perhaps you have reason to believe that death will come very soon. You may be troubled, feeling uncertain or unready to leave. But since the overwhelming majority of our lives will be spent on the other side of death, not this side, shouldn't we be careful to get ready for what awaits us there?

Make sure of your relationship with Jesus Christ. Be certain that you trust only him to save you—not anyone or anything else, and certainly not any good works you've done. And then allow yourself to get excited about what's on the other side of death's door.

Life becomes different when we realize that death is a turnstile, not a wall, and that our funerals will mark a small end and a great beginning. My friend Calvin Miller put it beautifully:

I once scorned ev'ry fearful thought of death,
When it was but the end of pulse and breath,
But now my eyes have seen that past the pain
There is a world that's waiting to be claimed.
Earthmaker, Holy, let me now depart,
For living's such a temporary art.
And dying is but getting dressed for God,
Our graves are merely doorways cut in sod.[108]

What can you learn from Reepicheep the mouse? From Emily and her mother? Why not ponder their stories and Calvin Miller's poem throughout this day, and see what encouragement they bring.

God, infuse us with a biblically based optimism. Help us to look beyond this brief life to the everlasting life that follows it in the world to come. Help us to make our daily choices now in light of eternity. Like Reepicheep, give us a bold passion that steps out in faith, moving forward in our quest to follow you to Heaven itself. Comfort us with the knowledge that our loved ones who love you will join us in that world. Remind us that you have taken away the sting of death, that death is not a hole but a tunnel. Our graves are merely doorways cut in sod—doorways that lead directly to you. "This is eternal life: that they may know you, the only true God, and Jesus Christ, whom you have sent."[109]

DAY 50

IT DOESN'T GET ANY BETTER THAN THIS... OR DOES IT?

Everyone who has this hope fixed on Him purifies himself, just as He is pure. — 1 JOHN 3:3, NASB

To come to Thee is to come home from exile, to come to land out of the raging storm, to come to rest after long labour, to come to the goal of my desires and the summit of my wishes.[110]
— CHARLES H. SPURGEON

If a bride-to-be has a wedding date on her calendar, and she thinks daily of the person she's going to marry and contemplates his qualities, then she shouldn't be an easy target for seduction, should she?

When I meditate on Jesus and my future in Heaven, sin is unappealing. It's when my mind drifts from that person and that place that sin seems attractive. Thinking of Heaven leads inevitably to pursuing holiness. Our high tolerance for sin testifies to our failure to prepare for Heaven.

Heaven should affect our activities and ambitions, our recreation and friendships, and the way we spend our money and time. If I believe I'll spend eternity in a world of unending beauty and adventure, will I be content to spend all my evenings playing video games or staring at game shows, sitcoms, and ball games? Even if I keep my eyes away from impurities, how much time will I want to invest in what ultimately doesn't matter?

When we realize the pleasures that await us in God's presence, we can forgo lesser pleasures now. When we realize the possessions that await us in Heaven, we will gladly give away possessions on Earth to store up treasures in Heaven. When we realize the power offered to us as rulers in God's Kingdom, a power we could not handle now but will handle with benevolence then, we can forgo the pursuit of power here.

Following Christ is a call not to *abstain* from gratification but (sometimes) to *delay* gratification. More to the point, it's a call to *pursue* the gratification that will last. It's finding our joy in Christ, rather than seeking joy in the things of this world. Heaven, the place of eternal gratification and fulfillment, should be our polestar, reminding us where we are and which direction we need to go.

To be Heaven-oriented is to be goal-oriented in the best sense. Paul says, "One thing I do: Forgetting what is behind and straining toward what is ahead, I press on toward the goal to win the prize for which God has called me heavenward in Christ Jesus" (Philippians 3:13-14).

Thinking of Heaven will motivate us to live each day in profound thankfulness to God: "Since we are receiving a kingdom that cannot be shaken, let us be thankful, and so worship God acceptably with reverence and awe" (Hebrews 12:28).

In *Perelandra*, C. S. Lewis's protagonist says of his friend Ransom, recently returned from another planet, "A man who has been in another world does not come back unchanged."[111] A man who gives sustained thought to another world—the Heaven where Christ is and the resurrected Earth where we will live forever with him—also does not remain unchanged. He becomes a new person.

The most ordinary moment on the New Earth will be greater than the most perfect moments in this life—those experiences you wanted to bottle or hang on to but couldn't. Nanci and I have spent some wonderful moments with our family and friends. At Christmas or on vacation, or simply after dinner in the family room, we've said those magic words: "It doesn't get any better than this." But it *can* get better, far better, than this—*and it will*.

Life on this earth now is like going out in the cold, dragging in the wood, or shoveling the coal, with periodic moments of deep satisfaction and times of distress and profound loss. Life on the New Earth will be like sitting in front of the fire with the ones we love, basking in the warmth, laughing outrageously, dreaming of the adventures to come—and then going out and *living* those adventures together. We'll have no fear that life will ever end, that our God will abandon us, or that tragedy will descend like a dark cloud. We'll have no fear that dreams will be shattered or relationships broken.

Do you ever feel you have passed your peak? That your best days are behind you, and what's ahead is all in decline? If you know Jesus, you are not past your peak. In fact, the further you drop from your earthly peak, the closer you get to Heaven. Death is the doorway to see Christ, who has defeated death and will swallow it up. Therefore, paradoxically, to be headed toward death is to be headed in the right direction.

Understanding that our peak doesn't come in this life should radically affect our view of deteriorating health. The elderly and disabled should recognize that their experiences on the New Earth will be far better than the best they have experienced on this earth under the Curse.

People without Christ can only look back to when they were at their best, and know they will never regain it. Memories are all they have, and even those memories are fading. But Christians don't look back to the peak of their prowess. They look *forward* to it.

When we Christians sit in wheelchairs or lie in beds or feel our bodies shutting down, let's remind ourselves, "I haven't passed my peak. I haven't yet come close to it. The strongest and healthiest I've ever felt is only a faint suggestion of what I will experience as a resurrected being on the New Earth."

This isn't wishful thinking. This is the explicit promise of God.

If the ideas presented in this book were merely the product of my imagination, they would be meaningless. But here's what the apostle John recorded at the end of the Bible:

> Then I saw a new heaven and a new earth. . . . And I heard a loud voice from the throne saying, "Now the dwelling of God is with men, and he will live with them. They will be his people, and God himself will be with

It Doesn't Get Any Better Than This . . . or Does It?

> them and be their God. He will wipe every tear from their eyes. There will be no more death or mourning or crying or pain, for the old order of things has passed away." He who was seated on the throne said, "I am making everything new!" Then he said, "Write this down, for these words are trustworthy and true." (Revelation 21:1, 3-5)

These are the words of King Jesus. Count on them. Take them to the bank. Live every day in light of them. Make every choice in light of Christ's certain promise.

We were all made for a person and a place. Jesus is the person. Heaven is the place.

If you know Jesus, we'll be together in that resurrected world, with the Lord we love and with the friends we cherish. We'll embark together on the ultimate adventure, in a spectacular new universe awaiting our exploration and dominion. Jesus will be the center of all things, and joy will be the air we breathe.

And just when we think, *"It doesn't get any better than this"*—it will!

Whom could you comfort today with the thought that those who love Jesus will never pass their peaks? Why not call or visit or send a note today?

☩ *O God, infuse us with joy at the thought of being with you. Remind us of your promise of no more death or mourning or crying or pain. Remind us daily that you will wipe every tear from our eyes. Help us to find precious hope in your vow to make everything new and in your assurance that your words are trustworthy and true. Help us to trust you today, rehearsing your promise of a better world. Help us to know, even on our best of days, that it will get better than this. Far better. And you, all-knowing and all-powerful God, will see to it that the far better world will never end.*

AFTERWORD
Living Now in Light of the World That Awaits Us

Do not let your hearts be troubled. Trust in God; trust also in me. In my Father's house are many rooms; if it were not so, I would have told you. I am going there to prepare a place for you. And if I go and prepare a place for you, I will come back and take you to be with me that you also may be where I am. — JOHN 14:1-3

I must keep alive in myself the desire for my true country, which I shall not find till after death; I must never let it get snowed under or turned aside; I must make it the main object of life to press on to that other country and to help others to do the same.[112] — C. S. LEWIS

Jesus promised that he was going to prepare a place for us, a place where we will live with him forever. The Heaven we go to when we die is part of what he has prepared, but it is not our final destination, just as the airport where we wait for a flight is part of our trip but not our destination. Where we're really going, the location of our eternal home, is the New Earth.

What kind of place can we expect our Lord to have prepared for us? Because he isn't limited, the possibilities are endless. I'm confident we can expect to find the best accommodations ever made by anyone, for anyone, in the history of the universe. The God who commends hospitality will not be outdone in showing hospitality to his children, whom he delights to comfort and reward.

A good carpenter envisions what he wants to build. He plans and designs. Then he does his work, carefully and skillfully, fashioning it to exact specifications. He takes pride in the work he's done and delights in showing it to others. And when he makes something for his bride or his children, he takes special care and delight.

Jesus is the carpenter from Nazareth. Carpenters know how to make things, and they know how to fix what's been damaged. Jesus has had experience building entire worlds (billions of them, throughout the universe). He's also an expert at *repairing* what has been damaged—whether people or worlds. And he's making a world for us, a remodel of the old Earth on a grand scale.

The Bible portrays life in God's presence, in our resurrected bodies in a resurrected universe, as so exciting and compelling that even the youngest and healthiest among us should look forward to it and daydream about it.

C. S. Lewis paints a beautiful picture of the eternal Heaven in *The Last Battle*, the final book of the Chronicles of Narnia. He concludes the series with what has become my favorite literary paragraph outside of Scripture:

> As [Aslan] spoke He no longer looked to them like a lion; but the things that began to happen after that were so great and beautiful that I cannot write them. And for us this is the end of all the stories, and we can most truly say that they all lived happily ever after. But for them it was only the beginning of the real story. All their life in this world and all their adventures in Narnia have only been the cover and the title page. Now at last they were beginning Chapter One of the great Story which no one on earth has read; which goes on for ever; in which every chapter is better than the one before.[113]

Think of it: The story isn't over when we die. The story isn't over when Christ returns. And the story isn't over even when God makes the New Earth and places us there to live forever. That's only the beginning.

When Lewis makes use of the standard fairy-tale ending—"they all lived happily ever after"—you might be tempted to say, "But fairy tales aren't true." However, Lewis's Chronicles allude to the Bible, which *isn't* a fairy tale. In fact, God's Word is utterly realistic, showing the worst in even its good characters. It is unswerving in its portrayal of sin and suffering. Nowhere in Scripture do we see naive, sentimental, wishful thinking. What we see is our devastating separation from God; our relentless sin; God's persistent faithfulness; the hard, grueling work of Christ's redemption; the tangible nature of his resurrection; and the promise of coming judgment. And, finally, we see the restoration of God's ideal universe, fulfilling his plan of the ages, which will culminate in resurrected people living with him on a resurrected Earth.

Then, and only then, will we live happily ever after.

By God's grace, I know that what awaits me in his presence, for all eternity, is something so magnificent it takes my breath away even as I write these words. Job declares it: "In my flesh I will see God. . . . I, and not another" (Job 19:26-27). That hope, that promise of redemption and restoration, eclipsed all of Job's heartaches. Surely it can eclipse yours and mine.

Think of it: Jesus, at unfathomable cost to himself, purchased for us a happy ending. A happy "ending" that will never end.

If you believe this, you won't cling desperately to this life. You'll stretch out your arms in anticipation of the greater life to come. Don't rob yourself of joy by letting even a single day go by without anticipating the new world that Christ is preparing for us.

If you don't yet know Jesus, it's not too late. Confess your sins and humbly accept the gift of his atoning sacrifice on your behalf. If you do know him, make your daily decisions in light of your destiny. By God's grace, use the time you have left on the present Earth to store up for yourself treasures on the New Earth, to be laid at Christ's feet for his glory (Revelation 4:10).

Knowing that this present world will end and become new heavens and a New Earth should profoundly affect your behavior. "You ought to live holy and godly lives as you look forward to the day of God. . . . In keeping with his promise we are looking forward to a new heaven and a new earth, the home of righteousness. So then, dear friends, since you are looking forward to this, make every effort to be found spotless, blameless and at peace with him" (2 Peter 3:11-14).

If we grasp the meaning of "a new heaven and a new earth," we *will* look forward to it. (And if we're not looking forward to it, it's because we simply *do not* comprehend it.) Anticipating our homecoming ought to motivate us to live spotless lives here and now. Anticipating our future on a resurrected Earth can empower us to persevere in a difficult marriage, remain faithful to the hard task of caring for an ailing parent or child, or stick with a demanding job. Moses remained faithful to God because "he was looking ahead to his reward" (Hebrews 11:26).

Jesus tells us that one day his faithful servants will hear their Master say, "Well done, good and faithful servant. You have been faithful over a little; I will set you over much. Enter into the joy of your master" (Matthew 25:23, ESV).

The idea of entering into the Master's joy is a telling picture of Heaven. It's not simply that being with the Master produces joy in us, though certainly it will. It's that our Master himself is joyful. He takes joy in himself, in his children, and in his creation. His joy is contagious. Heaven's environment is pure joy. Joy will be the very air we breathe. The Lord is inexhaustible—therefore his joy is inexhaustible.

Think about those incredible words: "Well done, good and faithful servant. . . . Enter into the joy of your master." Memorize those words. They are the words we *long* to hear, the words we were *made* to hear.

What changes do you need to initiate *today* so that you may one day hear those words from God?

Once we're home in Heaven, none of us will ever die again. Or suffer again. Or stay awake long lonely nights clutching the pillow next to us, wishing a loved one were still there. As a Christian, the day I die will be the best day I've ever lived. But it won't be the best day I *will* ever live. Resurrection day will be far better. And the first day on the New Earth—that will be one *big* step for mankind, one giant leap for God's glory!

I need to say something to readers who are battling serious depression. The fact that Heaven will be wonderful shouldn't tempt us to take a shortcut to get there. If you're depressed, you may imagine that your life has no purpose. But as long as God keeps you here on Earth, it's *exactly* where he wants you. He's preparing you for another world. He knows precisely what he's doing. Through your suffering, difficulty, and depression, he's expanding your capacity for eternal joy.

Our lives on Earth are a training camp to ready us for Heaven. Don't make a terrible ending to your life's story—finish your God-given course on Earth. When God is done—and not before—he'll take you home in his own time and way. Meanwhile, he has a purpose for you here on Earth. Don't desert your post. (And by all means, go to a Christ-centered, Bible-believing church and find a wise Christian counselor.)

If all this about the present Heaven and the New Earth seems more than you can imagine, I'd encourage you not to reject it on that basis.

Our God, after all, is called the one "who is able to do immeasurably more than all we ask or imagine" (Ephesians 3:20). The very next verse gives praise to this God who acts immeasurably beyond our imaginations: "To him be glory in the church and in Christ Jesus throughout all generations, for ever and ever!"

That's just what those of us who know Jesus will be doing forever: glorifying God, ruling the New Earth, beholding God's wonders in the magnificence of his new creation. Seeing God's face, we will spend the coming ages learning more and more of his grace and kindness.

I can hardly wait!

How about you?

WHAT MANY PEOPLE ASSUME ABOUT HEAVEN	WHAT THE BIBLE SAYS ABOUT HEAVEN
Non-Earth	New Earth
Unfamiliar	New, and old improved
Disembodied (Platonic)	Embodied (resurrected)
Foreign (utterly different from the home we know)	Home (all the comforts of home, with many innovations)
Leaving behind what we love	Retaining the good; finding the best ahead
No time and space	Time and space
Static, unchanging	Dynamic, developing
No art, culture, or progress	Art, culture, and progress
Neither old (like Eden) nor new and earthlike; just unknown and inhuman	Both old and new, familiar and innovative; nostalgia and adventure
Nothing to do but float on clouds and strum harps; old life and relationships forgotten	God to worship and serve; friends to enjoy; a universe to rule; purposeful work to do
Instant and complete knowledge, no curiosity; no learning or discovery	An eternity of exciting learning and discovery of God and his creation
Boring	Fascinating
Inhuman; no individuality; desires lost	Fully human individuals; desires fulfilled
Absence of the terrible (but the presence of little we desire)	Presence of the wonderful (everything we desire and nothing we don't)
Story over	Story continuing forever

NOTES

1. Anthony A. Hoekema, *The Bible and The Future* (Grand Rapids: Eerdmans, 1979), 50–54.
2. Ulrich Simon, *Heaven in the Christian Tradition* (London: Wyman and Sons, 1958), 218.
3. C. S. Lewis, *The Weight of Glory and Other Addresses,* revised and expanded edition (New York: Macmillan, 1980), 3–4.
4. Ola Elizabeth Winslow, *Jonathan Edwards: Basic Writings* (New York: New American Library, 1966), 142.
5. "Loving the Church," audiotape of sermon by C. J. Mahaney at Covenant Life Church, Gaithersburg, Md., n.d.
6. C. S. Lewis, *Mere Christianity* (New York: Collier, 1960), 118.
7. Gerhard Kittel and Gerhard Friedrich, eds., Geoffrey W. Bromiley, trans. and ed., *Theological Dictionary of the New Testament* (Grand Rapids: Eerdmans, 1964–76), 2:288.
8. Lewis, *Mere Christianity*, 118.
9. Francis Schaeffer, *Art and the Bible* (Downer's Grove, Ill.: InterVarsity, 1973), 61.
10. Ephesians 3:20.
11. John Donne, *Sermons III.*
12. Jonathan Edwards, *The Sermons of Jonathan Edwards: A Reader*, ed. Wilson H. Kimnach, Kenneth P. Minkema, and Douglas A. Sweeney (New Haven, Conn.: Yale University Press, 1999), 74–75.
13. Ibid.
14. Augustine, *The City of God*, 22, 30 and *Confessions* 1, 1, quoted in John E. Rotelle, *Augustine Day by Day* (New York: Catholic Book Publishing, 1986).

15. Augustine, *The City of God*, quoted in Alister McGrath, *A Brief History of Heaven* (Malden, Mass.: Blackwell, 2003), 182–183.
16. C. S. Lewis, *Letters to Malcolm: Chiefly on Prayer* (New York: Harcourt, 1963), 76.
17. K. Connie Kang, "Next Stop, the Pearly Gates . . . or Hell?" *Los Angeles Times*, October 24, 2003.
18. Ruthanna C. Metzgar, from her story "It's Not in the Book!" Used by permission. For the full story in Ruthanna's own words, see Eternal Perspective Ministries, http://www.epm.org/articles/metzgar.html.
19. Anthony A. Hoekema, "Heaven: Not Just an Eternal Day Off," *Christianity Today* (June 6, 2003).
20. McGrath, *A Brief History of Heaven*, 5.
21. Wayne Grudem, *Systematic Theology: An Introduction to Biblical Doctrine* (Grand Rapids: Zondervan, 1994), 1158.
22. George Sweeting and Donald Sweeting, "The Evangelist and the Agnostic," *Moody Monthly* (July/August 1989), 69.
23. St. Cyprian, *Mortality*, chapter 26.
24. Peter Toon, *Heaven and Hell: A Biblical and Theological Overview* (Nashville: Nelson, 1986), 26.
25. McGrath, *A Brief History of Heaven*, 40.
26. C. S. Lewis, *The Weight of Glory and Other Addresses* (Grand Rapids: Eerdmans, 1949), 13.
27. C. S. Lewis, *The Problem of Pain* (New York: Macmillan, 1962), 147.
28. Albert Wolters, *Creation Regained: Biblical Basics for a Reformational Worldview* (Grand Rapids: Eerdmans, 1985), 57.
29. Ibid., 58.
30. Philip P. Bliss, "Hallelujah, What a Savior!" *International Lessons Monthly*, 1875.
31. D. Martyn Lloyd-Jones, *Great Doctrines of the Bible* (Wheaton, Ill.: Crossway Books, 2003), part 3, 247–248.
32. Millard Erickson, *Christian Theology* (Grand Rapids: Baker, 1998), 1232.
33. Donald Guthrie, *New Testament Theology* (Downers Grove, Ill.: InterVarsity, 1981), 880.
34. Walton J. Brown, *Home at Last* (Washington, D.C.: Review and Herald, 1983), 145.
35. Paul Marshall with Lela Gilbert, *Heaven Is Not My Home: Learning to Live in God's Creation* (Nashville: Word, 1998), 247, 249.

36. Augustine, *The City of God*, Book XXII, chapter 29.
37. Richard Mouw, *When the Kings Come Marching In* (Grand Rapids: Eerdmans, 1983), 30.
38. In my summary of Isaiah 60, I am indebted to Richard Mouw's *When the Kings Come Marching In*.
39. A. A. Hodge, *Evangelical Theology: A Course of Popular Lectures* (Edinburgh: Banner of Truth, 1976), 399.
40. Ibid., 399–402.
41. Maltbie D. Babcock, "This Is My Father's World," 1901.
42. Revelation 22:3.
43. R. A. Torrey, *Heaven or Hell* (New Kensington, Pa.: Whitaker House, 1985), 68.
44. Anthony Hoekema, *The Bible and the Future* (Grand Rapids: Eerdmans, 1979), 251.
45. Westminster *Larger Catechism* (1647), question 87; http://www.reformed.org/documents/index.html?mainframe=http://www.reformed.org/documents/larger1.html.
46. The Westminster Confession of Faith, Chap. XXXI, "Of Synods and Councils," Presbyterian Church in America, http://www.pcanet.org/general/cof_chapxxxi-xxxiii.htm.
47. Joni Eareckson Tada, *Heaven: Your Real Home* (Grand Rapids: Zondervan, 1995), 39.
48. Erich Sauer, *The King of the Earth* (Grand Rapids: Eerdmans, 1962), 97.
49. Cornelius P. Venema, *The Promise of the Future* (Trowbridge, U.K.: Banner of Truth, 2000), 461.
50. Greg K. Beale, "The Eschatological Conception of New Testament Theology," *Eschatology in Bible and Theology*, ed. Kent E. Brower and Mark W. Elliott (Downer's Grove, Ill.: InterVarsity, 1997), 21–22.
51. Walter Bauer, *The Greek-English Lexicon of the New Testament and Other Early Christian Literature*, ed. Frederick W. Danker, 3rd ed. (Chicago: University of Chicago Press).
52. G. K. Chesterton, *Orthodoxy* (Chicago: Thomas More Association, 1985), 99–100.
53. Lewis, *Mere Christianity*, 120.
54. Marshall, *Heaven Is Not My Home*, 32–33.
55. Saint Teresa of Avila, *The Way of Perfection*, chap. 28, par. 2, Christian Classics Ethereal Library, http://www.ccel.org/ccel/teresa/way.i.xxxiv.html.
56. Irenaeus, *Heresies*, 5:32, 1 (SC 153:396–399).

57. Dallas Willard, *The Divine Conspiracy: Rediscovering Our Hidden Life in God* (San Francisco: HarperSanFrancisco, 1998), 378.
58. Matthew 25:23, ESV.
59. Willard, *The Divine Conspiracy*, 398.
60. McGrath, *A Brief History of Heaven*, 70.
61. C. S. Lewis, *The Last Battle* (New York: Collier, 1956), 169–171.
62. Isaiah 51:3.
63. Ezekiel 36:35, NASB.
64. John Wesley, Sermon 60, "The General Deliverance."
65. Ibid.
66. Augustine, *Confessions*, trans. H. Chadwick (Oxford: Oxford Press, 1991), 257.
67. Lewis, *Mere Christianity*, 190.
68. Grudem, *Systematic Theology*, 1158–1164.
69. Jonathan Edwards, *Heaven—A World of Love* (Amityville, N.Y.: Calvary Press, 1999), 24.
70. Colleen McDannell and Bernhard Lang, *Heaven: A History* (New York: Vintage Books, 1988), 307.
71. Dave Hunt, *Whatever Happened to Heaven?* (Eugene, Ore.: Harvest House, 1988), 238.
72. J. Boudreau, *The Happiness of Heaven* (Rockford, Ill.: Tan Books, 1984), 120–122.
73. Richard Baxter, *The Saints' Everlasting Rest* (1649).
74. Boudreau, *The Happiness of Heaven*, 107–108.
75. Victor Hugo, "The Future Life," quoted in Dave Wilkinson, "And I Shall Dwell," sermon preached at Moorpark Presbyterian Church, Moorpark, Calif., February 18, 20. See http://www.moorparkpres.org/sermons/2001/021801.htm.
76. St. Bede, from a sermon preached circa 710.
77. Salem Kirban, *What Is Heaven Like?* (Huntingdon Valley, Pa.: Second Coming, 1991), 8.
78. Boudreau, *The Happiness of Heaven*, 117.
79. George MacDonald, quoted in Herbert Lockyer, *Death and the Life Hereafter* (Grand Rapids: Baker, 1975), 65.
80. Amy Carmichael, "Thou Givest . . . They Gather," quoted in *Images of Heaven: Reflections on Glory*, comp. Lil Copan and Anna Trimiew (Wheaton, Ill.: Harold Shaw, 1996), 111.

81. W. Graham Scroggie, *What About Heaven?* (London: Christian Literature Crusade, 1940), 93–95.
82. Drake W. Whitchurch, *Waking from Earth: Seeking Heaven, the Heart's True Home* (Kearney, Neb.: Morris Publishing, 1999), 95.
83. Augustine, quoted in McDannell and Lang, *Heaven: A History*, 60.
84. Jim Elliot, quoted in Elisabeth Elliot, *Through Gates of Splendor* (Wheaton, Ill.: Tyndale, 1981).
85. *Babette's Feast*, directed by Gabriel Axel (Panorama Film, 1987).
86. Mouw, *When the Kings Come Marching In*.
87. Herman Bavinck, *The Last Things* (Grand Rapids: Baker, 1996), 160.
88. Mouw, *When the Kings Come Marching In*, 47.
89. Sam Storms, "Joy's Eternal Increase," in an unpublished manuscript on Jonathan Edwards's view of Heaven.
90. Hoekema, "Heaven: Not Just an Eternal Day Off."
91. Venema, *Promise of the Future*, 481.
92. Marshall, *Heaven Is Not My Home*, 30.
93. Ibid.
94. Ibid., 30–31.
95. Arthur O. Roberts, *Exploring Heaven* (San Francisco: HarperSanFrancisco, 2003), 148.
96. Piper, *Future Grace* (Sisters, Ore.: Multnomah, 1995), 381.
97. McDannell and Lang, *Heaven: A History*, 47.
98. Lewis, *The Last Battle*, 179.
99. James M. Campbell, *Heaven Opened: A Book of Comfort and Hope* (New York: Revell, 1924), 123.
100. Joni Eareckson Tada, quoted in Douglas J. Rumford, *What about Heaven and Hell?* (Wheaton, Ill.: Tyndale, 2000), 31.
101. Robert Browning, "Rabbi Ben Ezra," lines 1–3, in *Dramatis Personae* (London: Chapman and Hall, 1864).
102. Toon, *Heaven and Hell*, 204.
103. E. J. Fortman, S.J., *Everlasting Life after Death* (New York: Alba House, 1976), 309.
104. John Milton, quoted in Campbell, *Heaven Opened*, 75.
105. A poem variously attributed to Henry Scott Holland or Henry Van Dyke; source uncertain.

106. C. S. Lewis, *The Voyage of the "Dawn Treader"* (New York: Scholastic, 1952), 24.
107. Ibid., 180.
108. Calvin Miller, *The Divine Symphony* (Minneapolis: Bethany, 2000), 139.
109. John 17:3.
110. Charles H. Spurgeon, *Morning and Evening*, April 25, morning.
111. C. S. Lewis, *Perelandra* (New York: Simon & Schuster, 1996), 10.
112. Lewis, *Mere Christianity*, 120.
113. Lewis, *The Last Battle*, 228.

BOOKS BY RANDY ALCORN

FICTION

Deadline
Dominion
Deception
Edge of Eternity
Eternity
Lord Foulgrin's Letters
The Ishbane Conspiracy
Safely Home
Courageous
The Chasm

NONFICTION

Heaven
Touchpoints: Heaven
50 Days of Heaven
In Light of Eternity
Managing God's Money
Money, Possessions, and Eternity
The Law of Rewards
ProLife Answers to ProChoice Arguments
Sexual Temptation: Establishing Guardrails and Winning the Battle
The Goodness of God
The Grace and Truth Paradox
The Purity Principle
The Treasure Principle
Why Pro-Life?
If God Is Good
The Promise of Heaven
We Shall See God
90 Days of God's Goodness
Life Promises for Eternity
Eternal Perspectives
Everything You Always Wanted to Know about Heaven
hand in Hand

CHILDREN'S

Heaven for Kids
Wait Until Then
Tell Me about Heaven